Striking A Balance
Reflections On What Matters

Daniela Bryan

For information, contact:
DBCoach
info@dbcoach.com
www.dbcoach.com

ISBN: 978-0-9831668-0-1
A catalogue record for this title has been submitted to the Library of Congress.

Author: Daniela S. Bryan

Layout design: Chris Tandoc
Cover Design: Chris Tandoc
Copyeditor: Loretta Hudson
Proofreader: Loretta Hudson

Dedicated to Susie and Willy

May you have the strength of eagles' wings,
The faith and courage to fly new heights,
And the wisdom of the universe to carry you there.

Native American Blessing

ACKNOWLEDGMENTS

"Feeling gratitude and not expressing it is like wrapping a present and not giving it."
~*William Arthur Ward*

With much gratitude, I would like to acknowledge all who supported my work, encouraged my passion, and nudged me along, when I most needed it.

First, I want to thank my two children, Susie and Willy. Susie is an amazing writer and editor with deep insight. Willy has astute business sense and a good eye for design. Most of my learning comes through them. My friend, and our children's father, Ross Bryan, never ceases to support me any way he can. He remains a trusted friend. My dad trusts that I will do the *right* thing, even if he doesn't always approve. His guidance is priceless. My late mother continues to be my beacon and the best listener I have ever come across.

In addition to my family, I have been surrounded by a number of colleagues and friends who have inspired me and motivated me to strive further. A special thank you to Fred Andresen for his intellect and access to his resources, John Carter for his sense of humor and storytelling expertise, John Eaton for being a caring mentor, sounding board and friend, Susan Klein, for her focused coaching skills, and my unwaveringly supportive CAM sisters, Nancy Colasurdo, and Diane Krause-Stetson for being there, when I need an ear.

In order to make this book come alive, a number of professionals supported me in my quest. Thank you to Adina Siperman and Laura Friedlander, my virtual assistants; Loretta Hudson, my trusted editor; Chris Tandoc, my graphic designer; Brandon Steinweg, my Infusionsoft - Marketing Expert; and Mary Karlton and Peter Sterbach, who pointed me in the right direction.

Finally, thank you to all other family members and friends, colleagues, acquaintances and T-Birds that I haven't mentioned but who have contributed in meaningful ways to my path in the last ten years. You are in my heart...

TABLE OF CONTENTS

THE BEGINNING

Almost fifteen years ago, my life took a different path. Growing up in a Munich suburb, I had a very protected childhood. My father was a well-educated and well-traveled CEO. My mother was a well-educated woman who had chosen to stay home with her three children, not unusual in the 50s. Unusual, however, was the desire of mine to attend university in the United States of America. Hardly anyone went overseas for college education, especially girls. To have an impact on the world, and effect world peace, I thought I needed to pursue a career in international management, working for a multinational corporation. Naïve? Who was to know? I held on to that belief until I got burned out. I had a demanding job in the European Region Headquarter of the Eastman Kodak Company in London, working 60–80 hours a week, and traveling internationally every week. Living in Frankfurt, Germany, while working in London didn't exactly help. Being a Director of Marketing Communications and Training for one division responsible for Europe, Africa, and the Middle East was in many ways my dream job. After four years, it wasn't much fun anymore; something was missing. Instead of focusing on our careers, my husband and I decided to focus on family. Susie and Willy were born and brought sunshine into our hearts. I marveled at the growth and curiosity, the delight, but also the exhaustion that came with the new responsibility. I wanted to be present, watching this miracle unfold and decided to stay home with the children at least until they went to school. I quit my job at Kodak and we put down roots in California, where my husband was from. Living in a small beach town, after the hustle and bustle of London and Frankfurt, felt like starting over, like learning how to talk and walk all over again. Everything was exciting and new. I saw the world through my children's eyes as well as my own. I felt content, thinking I had gotten my travel bug out of my system before they were born.

But I knew I wanted to make a bigger impact. I loved working with people from different cultures. And I missed the interaction on a professional level. Relying on my training background, I decided to start my own business as a professional coach. People didn't seem to know what a coach really did, and I would argue coaching is still widely misunderstood in many people's minds. I think of myself as the sounding board everyone needs from time to time, providing outside perspective. With empathy and compassion, I challenge my clients to step outside of their comfort zones and break the patterns set forth by their limiting beliefs. I partner with my clients as they go through major transitions and when they need to make tough decisions in challenging times. Having had an international career myself, I am able to relate to challenges my international clients face. As much as they are growing, I am growing by listening to them. As much as my children are growing, I am growing right beside them. What fills me with joy is when I hear of my clients and my children, in turn, coaching their peers and community members.

This book entails a collection of anecdotes and stories of what I have learned along the way. You will notice that the book is divided into 4 sections, Work/Career, Money, Relationships and Emotional Well-Being. I believe, one can only find one's balance, by having addressed each of these areas equally.

Striking A Balance: Reflections On What Matters is what life is all about: Finding that inner equilibrium by reflecting on what is most meaningful, and important, to oneself.

What I want for you is to be inspired, motivated, challenged, and moved to reflect, take action for yourself, and embark on this inner journey with curiosity and excitement.

HOW TO USE
THIS BOOK

Striking A Balance: Reflections On What Matters is a collection of anecdotes, tips and reflections. The book can be used as

a) A thought-provoking read
b) A workbook, where action is taken after each chapter
c) A companion where randomly, a chapter is picked to spark reflection and inspiration.

All the lessons are universal and, I believe, can be applied anywhere, at any time.

At the end of the book, links to resources for immediate impact are available.

Note from the Author:
In order to make the material more readable, I randomly chose male and female, rather than writing he/she, him/her, etc.

WORK/CAREER

YOU, INC.

"A good name, like good will, is attained by many actions."

~ Author Unknown

Chief Executive Officers are leaders. What qualities make a good CEO? Vision, expertise, and leadership. Aren't those the qualities you need to lead a successful and productive life that is meaningful as well? As it turns out, it's time for you to give yourself a promotion, unless you already have that title (in which case, it's time to step it up). Go ahead, try it on:

Your Name

CEO

Your Name, Inc.

You are CEO, CIO, COO, CFO, CVO—and any of the Cs you can think of—all wrapped into one. You might outsource some of these functions, by having your taxes done by a CPA or by having a computer consultant who keeps you going on a technical level. You might have a housekeeper, maybe an executive assistant. It's time for you to elevate yourself so you can focus on what matters most. Once you have promoted yourself, it's time to celebrate. And, guess what? CEOs hire coaches to stay on track, to use as sounding boards, to stay focused, and to gain clarity. Why not you, too?

Incidentally, I like the title of Chief Listening Officer. Great CEOs are first, and foremost, great listeners. Listening is a key attribute of a leader and of great leadership. You might have noticed that my title is Chief Vision Officer. I hold this title because I see it as my contribution to hold the vision, and the various perspectives, that my clients have come to expect.

Reflections:

What title speaks to you?

What special contributions do you bring to your work?

What is expected of you in your job title?

FOLLOWING YOUR DREAM

"To look backward for a while is to refresh the eye, to restore it, and to render it the more fit for its prime function of looking forward."

~ Margaret Fairless Barber, *The Roadmender*

Kelly came to me distressed and disillusioned about her work, and life. At the time, she was working for an automobile manufacturer in Southern California. She was on the international business side introducing products to the Latin American market, and worked endless hours. Kelly's life was focused on work, work, and more work! Occasionally, she sprinkled in dinners, and drives in the countryside, with her husband. They sometimes fit in a short walk through the neighborhood with their dog. Kelly missed balance in her life, she missed her family in the Midwest, and there was no time for friends. She was very accomplished in her field, but her work wasn't fulfilling anymore.

Initially, we worked on reestablishing a balance between her work time and her private time. We focused on setting boundaries and scheduling what mattered most to her. We discovered her needs, her values, and her dreams. We started aligning her goals with her values. Through powerful questions asked as part of the coaching process, we peeled back the layers of beliefs that had made Kelly think that she couldn't do anything to change her current situation. By giving perspective and challenging her assumptions, I was able to help Kelly see what was possible. She could quit. And she could move to a different environment. She had many choices. Kelly did lots of research along the way to successfully make the transition. Kelly opened the doors of her new business, a day spa in

Tucson, Arizona—an all new way to experience a spa, with a mix-your-own treatment bar, and shelves full of bath and body products for customers to create their own bliss, in the store, or at home. The grand opening was a huge success and a milestone to be celebrated.

Kelly had recognized that she wanted to be an entrepreneur; innovative, and supportive of men and women in their quest to feel good about themselves. Her marketing savvy enabled her to open a retail store, a website, her own product line, and to market various products and services. She continued to take time off for waterskiing trips and to spend time with her family back home in Lake Michigan. Her dream was to eventually franchise her business concept. She has already made great connections toward realizing that dream.

Kelly has never lost sight of her ultimate goal—to live life to the fullest. She was ready to move forward on her own.

Recently, I received the following email from her:

Hi Dany!

I just had to send you a note and tell you about my exciting adventure. I landed a position with a major European fragrance house—their global scent marketing division and one of the most prestigious groups in the perfume industry. I'm off to NY for a six-month assignment that will very likely become full time, as well as to continue working on the side with my wine aromas. This job is the most perfect fit ever with my values, and it's international. I am glowing—all that I have done with Salud for the past several years has taken me to this, and I never would have dreamed it.

I came so close to taking a job in the auto industry, going back to the easy and familiar, but this scented path just unfolded like this because I was focused and knew what I really wanted. I'm sipping champagne, celebrating. Thank you so much for being here on this path helping me!!!

Always,
Kelly

Since then Kelly received a full-time job offer after only four weeks. She is also engaging in opportunities with potential investors and business growth for Salud. Way to go Kelly!

Reflections:
What in this story resonates with you?
What dream is unfulfilled for you?

GROWTH VERSUS NO GROWTH

"It is never too late to be what you might have been."

~ George Eliot

I am inspired to write about growth after having read the book *Small Giants—Companies That Choose to Be Great Instead of Big*, by Bo Burlingham, especially compared to *Good to Great* by Jim Collins.

In his book *Good to Great*, Jim Collins analyzes what makes a public company great. On the other hand, Burlingham, in *Small Giants*, analyzes the success of privately held companies and why they have chosen to not grow on purpose. I guess *bigger is not better* applies here.

Burlingham identifies seven common threads that led these companies to success, despite the conscious decision not to strive for growth. Let me paraphrase these:

1. Look at all possibilities, and don't follow the usual definition of success. It's better to be great than big.
2. Chart your own course and build a business you want to live with. Invent what works for you.
3. Create an intimate relationship with your local city, town, or county—a win/win between company and community.
4. Create an intimate relationship with your customers and suppliers. Under-promise and over-deliver, emphasizing personal contact.
5. Create an intimate workplace where creative, emotional, spiritual, social, and economic needs are addressed.
6. Create a business structure and mode of governance that work for you.

7. Nurture your emotional attachment to the business, the people that work within it, as well as the customers and suppliers. Let your passion shine through.

The companies described in the book, Anchor Brewing, Clif Bar & Company, and Union Square Hospitality, were successful in resisting pressures by employees, customers, and society at large. Above all, they charted their own course, often against conventional wisdom. What struck me in reading this book was that the founders, and owners, of these companies trusted their own instincts. They let their own inner wisdom tell them which path to take. If a decision allowed them to grow, but not take them on a path where they themselves wanted to be, or what they wanted for their employees or customers, they chose to say *no.*

I think this principle applies equally to our personal lives as to business. Personal and business growth is great as long as it is aligned with where you want to be. But as soon as you follow a path simply because you think you should be there, growth won't lead you to success.

I highly recommend Burlingham's book for any entrepreneur and for executives in leadership roles.

Reflections:
Who am I? What is most important to me?
Where am I personally, professionally, with my business?
Where do I want to be? What is driving me?
What actions do I need to take to get there?
What are the consequences if I decide pro growth? What are the consequences, if I decide against growth?

BEING WHO YOU WANT TO BE

"The future belongs to those who believe in the beauty of their dreams."

~ Eleanor Roosevelt, *Letters of Eleanor Roosevelt*

Because our economy is slow, and the job market is tight, many of my clients are concerned about making career changes and searching for jobs. So, I often try to address the whole area of career/job searches—how to make a resume quantifiable and measurable, how to use action words, how to make the résumé a great reflection of my client, how to network and connect with people, and how to interview for that dream job. But writing résumés and sending them out to prospective employers reflects only a small part of the process, the *doing* and not the *being*. The question is: "Who do we have to *be* to get/have our dream job?"

Many people I speak with are angry, fearful, apathetic, and unmotivated—in short, unhappy—in their current work environment. They spend energy and time worrying either about losing their present jobs or getting new, better jobs. They worry about their performance on their jobs, and the performance of other people on the job. "My company is down-sizing, and I am worried about my job. Am I going to be next?," "I hate my boss. Why is she so hard to work with?" "The job market is so tight. I feel stuck."

These individuals are usually looking outside of themselves for the answers to their work issues. Complaining along the way to family and friends, they wait for the company, or the boss, to change something or to decide their fate. Even those who take the leap, and move on to different jobs often find themselves in the same unhappy dilemma.

If you are unhappy in your work, you are the only one with the power to make a change. It is not up to your company, boss, spouse, or co-worker to make your life better or provide you with job satisfaction. It is your responsibility and your choice! It is difficult to find a truly satisfying job, no matter how much money it pays or how influential the job seems, unless you look inside yourself and connect with who you are and what your gifts are.

Reflections:
Look within yourself and find your passion, what you truly love, what brings you joy. Then be willing to have the courage to make some changes so you can create work that not only pays the bills, but also is an expression of who you are. Concentrate on the *being*, not the *doing*! You'll never again settle for second best.

ARE YOU ASKING YOURSELF MEANINGFUL QUESTIONS?

"Some of the best lessons we ever learn are learned from past mistakes.
The error of the past is the wisdom and success of the future."

~ Dale E. Turner, American Journalist

I often ask my clients at the end of a project: *What were the lessons learned? Would you do it again? If so, what would you do differently?* Having renovated a barn into a home, I learned four lessons. These lessons can be adapted to any life situation, such as career planning or building a business. They seem so simple, and yet they are not so easy to implement. Take a look:

1. Define your vision, and stick with it

From the beginning of my project I wanted to build a barn overlooking a prairie and forests that I could live and work in, simply, but very comfortably. Guess what—I got just that. But it wasn't easy to realize this vision. Every step along the way, choices had to be made—lots of choices! Each decision would have been much harder to make if I hadn't had a vision of the finished product in my head. I had to give myself permission to say no to distractions. I let my vision guide me. I could feel the finished product. I could sense it. I believe that's the reason why my barn felt like home from the day I moved in.

What is your vision for your business, your career, and your vocational path?

2. Expect the unexpected

This is true, especially regarding finances. I created a budget and had a large contingency budget. My barn isn't exactly a tract house, so foreseeing how much everything was going to cost was next to impossible, for myself as well as for my advisors, such as my contractor and architect. Nobody could have known that there would be more than the normal rainfall that year, resulting in the need for a more substantial reconstruction of the driveway than I had anticipated. Certain items were more expensive, others less. Forecasting is always a guess and an educated guess at best. So expect the unexpected.

What is your budget? How much of a contingency did you build in? What are the consequences if you have to tap into your reserves?

3. Enjoy the journey

I have been asked if I would do it again. I won't deny that it was a lot of work and that it was stressful at times. But it was also a great deal of fun. I learned about materials, timing, money, how to work with contractors. The list goes on. Bottom line: it was fun, and I was sad not to see the various contractors anymore after working with them so closely for months. Yes, it felt good to be done and to have reached the goal, but I enjoyed myself along the way as well.

What about you? Are you enjoying your current job? Is it fun growing your business? If not, what needs to change? What do you need to do differently?

4. Surround yourself with a great team

My contractor was awesome. Yes, there were issues to deal with, there were compromises and delays, and, yes, there was bad news at times. Still, I trusted my contractors and respected their opinions. After all, they are experts in their field. So, why shouldn't I have trusted them?

What about your team? What team do you have in place to see your vision out to the end? Do you trust your financial advisors, your mortgage broker, your accountant, and your insurance agent? Are all of you on the same wavelength? We surround ourselves with advisors in each area of our lives. Why not the best? What stops you from taking inventory of your team? Do you trust your team members, and do you respect them? Are they available when you need them the most?

Reflections:
Would I do it again? In a flash!
Would I do it differently? Not significantly!
Am I satisfied with the outcome? Totally!

WHAT PATTERNS ARE HOLDING YOU BACK?

"Life is like an ever-shifting kaleidoscope—a slight change,
and all patterns alter."

~ Sharon Salzberg

"I have a great job in an industry I thought I wanted to be in, but I am miserable. Part of that misery may have to do with a verbally abusive manager, but I am beginning to think this industry isn't for me," John said to me. He had hired me as his coach and we had worked together to strengthen his personal foundation by identifying his needs and values. He began to shift from being the victim to having the courage to express what he needed and to take action. He found the power in himself to quit his job by trusting that he would do well no matter what would happen next. The result was that he obtained the funding for a new business idea, won a trip around the world, and received a job offer upon his return from that trip. He is now happily employed in the same industry, but working for a different company.

"I need focus and a feeling that I am moving in the right direction, which is certainly lacking right now," Kevin wrote in an email. He was unemployed at the time and quite frustrated with the job search in an increasingly challenging, and tight, job market. Through coaching, he learned how to take care of himself by allowing himself to travel, even though the money was tight. He managed to focus on his job search even while he was away. He went from fearing rejection to actively pursuing possibilities and asking for what he wanted, which resulted in the renegotiation of a lease that saved him several thousand dollars. He shifted from spinning his wheels to seeking opportunities that resulted in many more job interviews. He learned that, rather than having to be self-sufficient, he could seek appropriate help and support. He realized that he is the only one who knows what's best for him, and that he often had taken comments during interviews, or rejection letters, personally. He began to trust himself more and to trust his intuition. He is now employed under a contract, so he is more autonomous, and free, than if he were fully employed.

"I say I want to leave my company, but that is such a scary proposition. But, in the back of my mind, I know, through this self-searching and awareness, I will most likely realize this corporate life never was—nor ever will be—for me. I guess I need some direction."

Kristie is still working for her company; however, she is discovering that many of her needs are not being met by her current position, and that she is not honoring her values. "I want to *do* something rather than just talk about it." Coaching helped her become aware that the work she was doing every day didn't seem to have a purpose. Currently, she is making active changes while finding purpose in her work.

As a personal and professional coach, I work with people in transition, by helping them focus on what's most important to them, by helping them make better decisions, and by supporting them to say *yes* to themselves and *no* to what's dragging them down.

All three of the clients mentioned above are in various stages of career transitions. Whether you want to move up or out, the following strategies will help you move forward, especially when you are in a career transition:

1. Look in the mirror

Are you doing something you love? Is your life working? Are you still challenged professionally and personally? Look at yourself first, not at the jobs out there.

2. Strengths

What are your strengths? Take inventory of your credentials, your skills and expertise, your relationships, your network, your track record, your overall life balance. The more clarity you have about your strengths, the easier it is to communicate them to others.

3. Career/life plan

Do you know what you want in your life/career? What are your values? What do you want to create in the next 10 years? Getting clear on what you want will help you make a better career move.

4. Opportunities and possibilities

Keep track of your successes and achievements, and translate them into opportunities and possibilities. Have you done workshops and presentations before? How can you leverage them?

5. Simplify

Clean out the clutter and release things you no longer love, or need, in your physical environment and also in your emotional environment, your relationships, and your career.

6. Surround yourself with people you respect and admire

Find people who are successful in their careers, and their lives, to be models for you. You have a choice about whom you surround yourself with. Be open to learn from these people.

7. Take action
Do something rather than complain or talk about it. The choice is yours. Take initiative. Be in control.

8. Nurture your network
This is the time to reconnect with people in your current network and establish new connections. Look at your areas of interest and areas of intentional growth, and look at ways you can expand your contacts, locally, statewide, nationally, or internationally.

9. Intuition
Trust your intuition and your gut-level feelings. If you feel some hesitation walking into an interview situation, ask yourself what's wrong. What do you need to do, or find out, to make it right?

10. The present is perfect
Transitions are opportunities for learning and growing. To better enjoy the journey, focus on the moment rather than on the past, or the future.

My clients are at different stages of their individual self-discovery. However, all of them realize they make the most progress in their transitions if they are willing to challenge their own behavior patterns and belief systems that have guided them in the past. With that in mind, what patterns or behaviors are you holding on to?

SABOTAGE?

"A journey of a thousand miles begins with a single step."

~ Lao-tzu, The Way of Lao-tzu

No matter how much you feel in control of your life, plans or events, sometimes things turn out differently than expected. You find yourself asking: Why did this happen to me? What am I doing wrong? This is so unfair! I wasn't anticipating this! How was I to know?

Setbacks in your professional life can be sudden and unexpected. But even minor setbacks can derail us. Yet, they are part of life. Of course we don't want any worries or challenges, but, as we grow older, more of them seem to be coming at us. However, whining and complaining about the fact that setbacks happen won't get you closer to your goals. Wishing things would be different is simply a waste of energy. Life is just not always fair!

When faced with a setback, you have every right to feel upset, angry, and frustrated. Give yourself permission to feel the full range of emotions you are having. Vent to your friends or family members, cry on someone's shoulder, or mourn the loss. Eventually however, it doesn't do you any good to stay stuck in your emotions. What steps do you need to take to move forward?

To turn a setback into a success, you need to ask yourself more constructive questions. *How could this have happened?* or *Why did this happen to me?* are questions that leave you feeling powerless and in despair. You are allowing yourself be a victim, and you are blaming something, or someone else, for the problem. These questions give you negative energy.

Positive energy comes from *what* or *I wonder how*, questions that open up new possibilities and solutions that empower you. Let me give you some examples:

OLD: "Why did this happen to me?"
NEW: "What can I learn from this?"
OLD: "Why me?"
NEW: "I wonder what I can do to overcome this hurdle?"

Can you feel the difference? Have you been asking yourself some of these *why* questions? Write down how you can rephrase them into positive *what* questions that empower you to move on.

Caution: Watch out for the *what if* pitfall: *What if I make a job change and it doesn't work out? What if I ask for a raise and get denied? What if I speak the truth, but it isn't received well?* Those questions get you stuck in a worst-case scenario, and they keep you stuck in a life you don't like. The result is you don't do anything, because *what if* something bad happens?

However, you can turn *what if* questions around to open up new possibilities. So let's try it: *What if you make a job change and you end up having your dream job? What if I ask for a raise and receive more than I expected? What if I speak the truth and it does get heard and acted upon?* Practice turning your negative *what ifs* into powerful possibilities!

You can't control most of the events that happen in your life. Setbacks are going to happen, whether you want them or not. Expect the unexpected. What you can control is the way you react to those events, and how you let them affect you. You always have choices about how to deal with things.

Give yourself the time to process a setback, but then begin to listen to the way you talk to yourself. Eliminate sabotaging self-talk, and begin to turn those thoughts around. Choose to be someone who looks at setbacks as opportunities to learn something new about yourself, and discover the strength you possess to overcome these hurdles. Everything does happen for a reason—sometimes it takes us a little bit longer to realize what that reason is!

GUILT-FREE VACATION

"No man needs a vacation as much as the man who just had one."

~ Elbert Hubbard

The dates have been on your calendar for a while. You are going on a trip – for business or pleasure. This starts what I call *the vacation syndrome*: As we get ready, we feel compelled to get everything done before we leave. It makes us feel better. As we clear our desks, even more things than usual seem to get added to our already busy calendars. It becomes increasingly difficult to say *no*. The notorious *should* creeps in. We *should* finish the report before we leave. We *should* meet with the clients or bosses before departing. We *should* show up to the office party—the list goes on. Let me make a distinction between *duty* and *obligation* that might help in deciding what needs to be taken care of.

There is a very fine line between *duty* and *obligation*. An *obligation* is externally driven and we feel responsible to take some action. A *duty* is something we *desire* to do, is internal, and nobody is telling us to do it. For example, we might feel obligated to work overtime, especially before a trip because it is our duty to keep the operation of our job/business going in our absence. *There is no need to complete the same amount of work before our trip that we would usually complete if we were not taking a vacation.* Instead of trying to get everything done, focus on informing, and delegating, to the people around you. Schedule meetings for when you return, rather than cramming the meeting in before you go. If you work with a to-do list, clearly mark what has to happen before you go, (remember, no "shoulds"), and schedule accordingly for when you return.

Make sure you have a backup person in place who can answer most questions in your absence, and let go of having to do it all yourself. Remember, whatever you don't get done before you go will either still be there when you return, or it wasn't important enough to get handled in the first place.

Reflections:
What has to get done by me before my departure?
What has to get done by someone else before my departure or
   during my absence?
What can wait until I get back?
What would make the time before my departure stress free?

WHAT RISK ARE YOU WILLING TO TAKE?

"Will you be the rock that redirects the course of the river?"

~ Claire Nuer, psychologist

We have all heard that putting all our eggs in one basket is extremely risky. If something happens to the basket, all the eggs are lost. If we observe others, we discover that many people are living with more risk than they think, or they are living with more risk than they had bargained for. If our livelihood is dependent on one source of income, such as a job, a real estate investment, or a portfolio, we are naturally taking on more risk than when our income sources are spread out. Some people think a diversified portfolio is enough to spread the risk, but, as it turns out, that's not true. If you work for someone else, you are dependent on others to give you something to do, and to keep you employed. You are not in charge of your destiny, and, as a result, you cannot manage your risk. The only way to spread the risk is by adding additional income sources through investing, publishing, or other means.

Interestingly, many people think an entrepreneur has more risk than an employee. However, the entrepreneur is in control of the risk. No one can fire him or her, and the risk can be managed by changing marketing strategies or by streamlining expenses. I believe the entrepreneur has less risk but more ambiguity, more uncertainty. No one can predict the future, but people feel safe when they take on a formal job. Unfortunately, it's a false sense of security, as too many are experiencing right now. Risk versus ambiguity: which one is right for you? Can you handle the unknown that comes with being an entrepreneur? Unknowns such as, what will the profit look like this month, next month, a year from now? Customers come, and customers go, and they have a direct impact on your bottom line. On the other hand, can you handle the risk of being without your salary from one day to the next?

In the current job market, many are unemployed and faced with worries about mortgages, bills, their children's college education, and their own retirement. I personally have always been in favor of diversification. Regardless, whether you work for someone else or you work for yourself, don't put all your eggs in one basket. The more you diversify, the less you will put yourself at risk. Uncertainty is something we have to live with no matter what. Who knows what tomorrow will bring? Unwavering faith will help us tread unknown waters. Faith in *what*, you might ask? Faith in *yourself* to do the right thing and make the right choices, and faith that the present is perfect—even if, at times, it doesn't seem that way.

Reflections:
What risk are you willing to tolerate?
What are your strategies to deal with uncertainty?
What do you believe about risk?

MANAGEABLE RISKS

"Take calculated risks. That is quite different from being rash."

~ George S. Patton, American General

I recently went on my son's year-end backpacking trip from school. I had gone on a similar trip with my daughter's class two years earlier. The trips, even though laid out equally, were quite different. Last time, my totem was a rattlesnake, which I wasn't thrilled with. I am really not very fond of snakes, even though I can appreciate their beauty. This time, my totem was a butterfly, actually lots of them. Wherever I looked, butterflies were all around me, all sorts of shapes and colors. I am grateful I was able to witness their peacefulness and grace. Something else that was different on this trip was the water level of the North Fork of the Merced River. (For those of you unfamiliar with California, the Merced River runs through Yosemite National Park. We were just east of the Park.) The area had so much rain and snow at the higher elevations that the snow really didn't start melting in significant amounts until the middle of May.

Rather than seeing tranquil ponds separated by huge rocks, we were facing rapids, and raging waterfalls. The kids loved it. We spent a significant amount of time in the water, which was great, considering the scorching outside temperature. One afternoon, we went on a river walk—no, not alongside, but *in* the river. It included rock hopping, climbing up waterfalls, and swimming through ponds. At one point we had to traverse the river by swimming through it. We could see the powerful current that transported leaves downstream at significant speed. The bravest of the group started to jump from a rock to shorten the distance between the two riverbanks. Before too long, all the kids had successfully crossed except for one girl. She was visibly frightened, and she didn't trust her own abilities to swim across the river. She clung to the rock and refused to budge. Between her classmates and the adults, we tried to cheer her on and convince her that she'd be fine. I actually think that the encouragement created more pressure. Everyone was watching her, so she froze. Some of her classmates came halfway back across the river and reached out to assist her. It was a good idea, and noble of her peers, but that didn't do the trick either. Nothing helped until our group leader, Kelly, swam over to her and said, "Robin, I am a good swimmer. I swam underneath the Golden Gate Bridge through shark-infested waters. How about if you climb on my back and I'll take you over?" The girl's face lit up. The look of relief was precious. And within seconds she was on the other riverbank and smiling. This particular scene stuck with me, as it can be applied to so many situations in business, and in life.

The risk of swimming across by herself was way too big for the girl. The risk was still too big when peers shortened the distance. But swimming across on someone's back was an acceptable risk level. Let's think of a business situation to apply this to. How about cold calling a potential customer? It's scary and doesn't promise much chance of success. But, if you know someone who can introduce you to the potential customer, the risk is minimized—then cold calling becomes more appealing.

How about when it comes to making a business investment? You spend the money, but you might not get anything in return. But, if you invest the money, and you can test the product/service for a while, the risk is reduced—the investment becomes more acceptable. The list goes on.

What challenges do you have that require you to take a risk? Ask yourself: *How can I reduce the risk? What will it take for me to find this risk acceptable?* Over time, you might become more daring and challenge yourself to more. You learn to trust yourself, and your instincts, more. You become more self-confident. We can all benefit from more self-confidence, and self-esteem.

Reflections:
Write down three situations in your life that require you to take a risk. How will you reduce the risk?

FLOW LIKE WATER

"To decide, to be at the level of choice, is to take responsibility
for your life and to be in control of your life."
~ Abbie M. Dale

I want to make a distinction between setting goals, and reaching goals, and being in the flow. Please note that *being in* the flow is not to be confused with *going with* the flow, which I will explain later. All of us set goals—a new job, a raise, a promotion. Goals come in all shapes and sizes. They mark a sense of accomplishment. We define what we want, we declare it to others around us, we work hard at reaching the goal, and we feel the sense of accomplishment when we finally reach the goal.

Sometimes, when we reach our goal, we feel the gratitude of having done it, but the process also leaves us exhausted. We feel that we had to work very hard to get there. We had to push ourselves to overcome obstacles. However, if we are in the flow, we are so pulled along by what we are doing that the path seems extremely effective and effortless. Success seems to just happen rather than us forcing ourselves to get there.

Flow was identified in long distance running, because, upon reaching a certain point, the running just seemed to take place without effort while the runner experienced an almost ecstatic state. This is true for many sports, and it also applies in business, and your personal life.

Let's say you want to attract new clients for your business. The more you push, the harder it seems to be able to attract new clients. But, by looking for opportunities rather than clients, and serving your existing clients with the highest level of integrity, you can get in the *flow*, which is attractive to potential clients. They can feel your ease. It then becomes effortless to get new clients.

Or, let's consider when you set out to get a promotion. The more you concentrate on the act of receiving the promotion, the less you concentrate on the quality of your work. But, by remaining positive and succeeding at all your job tasks, you get into the *flow* that will lead you to the next rung on the ladder.

Going with the flow will end up having you going along for the ride to reach someone else's goal. It rarely leads to personal satisfaction. *Being in* the flow will allow you to reach your own goals and desires.

Reflections:
What goals have you set for yourself?
What action will it take for you to reach your goals?
What will it take to make the journey effortless?
Who do you need to be?

WHAT IS YOUR ENTREPRENEURIAL LIFE PATH?

"I'm convinced that about half of what separates the successful entrepreneurs from the non-successful ones is pure perseverance."
~ Steve Jobs, Apple Computer CEO

I often write about shifting paradigms and how we need to solve problems from a higher level of consciousness. Old paradigms, such as the linear progression of school, college, and career, don't seem to work anymore. Many of my clients get to the point where the typical nine-to-five corporate job in a hierarchical organization no longer works for them. Much of my coaching is focused on dealing with that transition. People come to me because they feel stuck in a rut. They end up transitioning from a corporate work environment to starting their own business, allowing them more flexibility and freedom.

I recently came across a book called *Life Entrepreneurs—Ordinary People Creating Extraordinary Lives*, by Christopher Gergen and Gregg Vanourek. [See "Resources" section in the back of the book.] According to the authors: *People are looking for opportunity, challenge, and the chance to develop their talents, achieve success, and make an impact. But they are also looking for a rich home life, rewarding friendships, an active lifestyle, and deeper fulfillment. Life entrepreneurs are able to thrive in all these realms by proactively taking the following steps:*

Discovering Core Identity
Awakening the Opportunity
Envisioning the Future
Developing Goals and Strategies
Building Healthy Support Systems

Taking Action and Making a Difference
Embracing Renewal and Reinvention

I agree with all of these steps. The challenge lies in following through with all of them on a daily basis, when obstacles get in the way. Being a life entrepreneur requires being proactive and being disciplined, otherwise we either don't even get started or we get sidetracked—and distractions are everywhere. Above all, it requires us to really know who we are and to be willing, and able, to show up in our own life.

Life Entrepreneurs—Ordinary People Creating Extraordinary Lives gives a good foundation of what areas to look at. The stories cited are compelling and inspiring. And yet, a book doesn't give you a chance to talk through your thoughts, feelings, your concerns and desires, your inner most gremlins. That's why I love being a coach: I provide the space for my clients to think things through, to learn, to gain perspective, and to hear the truth. I give them permission to be who they are.

DREAMING BIGGER

"If one advances confidently in the direction of his dreams, and endeavors to live the life which he has imagined, he will meet with a success unexpected in common hours."
~ Henry David Thoreau, *Walden*

While reading a German weekly publication, I came across a prime example of a visionary, in fact, a couple of visionaries: Christo and Jeanne-Claude, the most famous artist couple of our time. You might recall the *Surrounded Islands* in Miami 1983, or the *Wrapped Reichstag*, Berlin, Germany in 1995, two examples of their visionary art pieces.

The Gates, in Central Park, New York is one of their most famous masterpieces. The project included 7,500 gates with saffron colored fabric panels weaving its way through New York's Central Park. The enormous art project stretched across 23 miles of walkways, using over 5,000 tons of steel and over 1,000,000 square feet of recyclable fabric. All the parts were dismantled and recycled after 16 days. Wow!

Anyone who can dream up an art project of this magnitude must have a vision, no doubt. In addition, I was astounded to read that they financed the entire project themselves. The cost of the project is over $21,000,000. Christo created over 400 sketches and collages to come to the final art installation. No grants, fundraising, or sponsors. Selling your artwork for $21 million is not an easy task. In a sense, he is selling a visual representation of his vision. Wow!

What impressed me above all, however, is the fact that the idea was created 26 years ago. The vision was there, the execution depended on many variables, including the right timing. If building this art project had been a goal, I doubt they would have been able to complete the task after 26 years, but a vision kept them on track and focused. They wanted to see this project come to life and building *The Gates* made their vision come to life. Wow!

Whether you like their work, or not, one can't help being impressed by the magnitude of their vision.

A vision beyond your wildest dreams, wouldn't that be a kick? You have always had your dream job. If *The Gates* teaches us anything, it is to stick to our vision – no matter how outlandish, no matter how impossible it may seem to others. Funding, doubts, fears, negativity cannot stand in your way when you have a vivid and direct goal. Each of us may become the Christo of our vision. To infinity and beyond!

CHOICES AND DECISIONS

"Truly successful decision making relies on a balance between
deliberate and instinctive thinking."
~ Malcolm Gladwell, *Blink*

When it comes to work, we make decisions every day – sometimes they are big decisions with potentially enormous consequences, and most often they are little decisions where the stakes aren't so high. Have you ever considered how you arrive at these decisions, and how you feel in the process? And what helps you arrive at the best decisions for your current situation? I have had many opportunities to observe the decision making process within groups, individuals, and within myself. Intuitively, I know the principles, but I enjoy observing the results in others and myself.

I had the privilege of accompanying a group of fourteen 5th graders on a backpacking trip into the California wilderness. What a remarkably capable group of children! They carried all their gear, they did all of the cooking and cleaning. They were adventurous, yet aware of the potential dangers of being out in the wild. On the last evening out, their challenge was to designate four leaders for various tasks to be completed the next day. (This scenario can easily be applied to any managerial setting in the corporate world. The same principles apply.) Some children had been leaders before and wanted to lead again. Others hadn't had the chance to lead, but wanted to give it a try. And some were quite happy being Indians rather than chiefs. What the group really struggled with was coming up with FOUR leaders. The choices were overwhelming. They either had too many leaders, or too few, and some group members got really frustrated. Some started yelling. Others completely quieted down. The decision making process had broken down after about 20 minutes of discussion! Being an observer and not involved in the discussion, I could see the dilemma. Earlier that day, the kids had competed with each other in a scavenger hunt as members of four groups. So, I suggested that they get back into the same groups and pick a group member to become part of the leadership team the next day. After only 2 minutes they decided on 4 competent leaders! Without making the decision for them, I had narrowed down the choices for them. They felt competent, and in control, and they arrived at a decision much quicker.

Sometimes we have too many options and the decision making process becomes overwhelming. We seem to feel more comfortable making decisions when given a limited number of choices.

At the other end of the spectrum, the decision-making process becomes frustrating when you are not given enough, or any, choices.

Recently, I walked out of my dentist's office frustrated, because I was simply told what procedure was to be performed and when. I wasn't given any options and felt very powerless, and out of control. The procedure might well have been the best one under the circumstances and, given that the dentist sees similar scenarios several times a week, perhaps other options didn't even occur to him. But I hadn't arrived at that decision, I wasn't even given the option. Clearly not having enough choices didn't work for me.

The question remains - what is the *right* amount of options? I haven't come across any scientific data, but based on my experience anywhere between 2 and 4. You might wonder why this is important. If you are faced with a decision, you might want to write out all your options. That way you can examine all end possibilities and make an educated, secure decision. As well, you may prevent yourself from feeling forced into only one option. Conversely, if you are a professional expecting decisions from your clients, customers or patients, you might want to consider offering an appropriate number of choices to empower, yet not overwhelm. If you are an executive in the corporate world you might want to think carefully about offering choices to your employees, peers, or your boss.

What decisions do you have to make right now? Do you feel overwhelmed by the task? Try to limit your options and see how things shift for you. You might want to solicit help from a friend, peer, or coach to limit your options for you.

Reflections:
What decisions are you expecting others around you to make? Have you given them any choices? Or maybe too many?

ARE YOU PREPARED TO SHIFT YOUR WAY OF THINKING?

"Your paradigm is so intrinsic to your mental process that you are hardly aware of its existence, until you try to communicate with someone with a different paradigm."

~ Donella Meadows, *The Global Citizen*

I was part of a conference call offered by the Newfield Network called *Paradigms - A Global Challenge*. The Newfield Network offers coach training and leadership development using onto-logical approaches to learning, in other words learning based on the philosophical study of the nature of being. Albert Einstein said: "No problem can be solved from the same level of consciousness that created it." Similarly, the discussion on the phone call centered around the notion that there has been a collective consciousness that has worked for mankind in the past, a consciousness that got us to where we are today, but that won't help us solve the problems from here on out.

The call was so affirmative of what I see happening in my work, that I feel compelled to share my thoughts with you.

When one looks at today's business organizations (for profit corporations, not for profits, and small companies), one can see their structure is like a pyramid. There is a chain of command leading to the top. This structure is based on the notion that in order to make decisions that affect everyone, an individual or governing body (i.e. CEO or Board of Directors) needs to have all the answers to the questions before them. With rap-idly expanding information technology this is an interesting challenge. How can one person know everything? What if the Board of Directors doesn't know either?

I am willing to argue that the best leaders are those who are willing to admit they don't know, and don't have, all the answers. In the past, at least in western culture, we looked at people as individuals. We are beginning to realize that, in fact, we are all connected. And technology is teaching us how to work with our connectivity. Just look at the success of social, and professional, networking sites. The answers to problems can come from within an organization, up and down the ladder, but they can equally well come from the outside. There is a tendency toward a more collaborative work style. If our connectedness is breaking open the paradigms of organizations, as we know them, what will organizations look like in the future?

We have already seen signs of where the traditional organization is changing. Just look at how the numbers of telecommuters has dramatically increased. Managers are resisting this trend for fear of losing control. They don't know what their telecommuting employees are doing and want to keep telecommuting to a minimum. We have also seen a shift in corporations to contract more work out rather than hire full-time employees. The advantage to the corporation lies in increased flexibility, and new ideas and expertise from the outside. Also, the younger generation entering the work force puts greater emphasis on work/life balance. They don't want to accept 60 - 80 hour workweeks, unlike the generation before them.

It seems to me in order to move toward this new consciousness we, as individuals and as organizations, need to let go of some established ways of doing things. For example: What if we were to let go of wanting to please investors with short-term earnings? What if we were to let go of some of the ways of measuring success? What if we let go of return on invest-ment and replace it with return on expectations? Patagonia, the outdoor clothing company, for example, is recognizing that their customers expect them to reduce their footprint on earth. Yes, ROI is important, but maybe we need to measure another return as well. What are the possibilities, if we were to let go of pyramidical organization structures? Can you imagine what an impact that would have on you, your family, your community, society at large, and the world? Can you imagine?

Thinking of the possibilities gives me goose bumps. Let's buckle up and enjoy the ride. Rather than being fearful of it, let's embrace it. It's up to all of us to create our new paradigm together.

Reflections:
What organizations are you a part of?
What shifts do you see happening in the organizations you are
a part of?
What are you observing about other organizations?
What can you incorporate?
What belief are you letting go of?

SUCCESSFUL FOLLOW UP

"Everyone has talent. What is rare is the courage to follow the talent to
the dark place where it leads."

~ Erica Jong, *author*

You've heard it before - In tough economic times, for business leaders and job searchers alike, the name of the game is networking. Whether you network actively or passively, networking is all about relationship building. Whether you are building relationships with business partners, potential employers, customers or prospects, making the initial contact is only the first step. All too often it remains the last step. Perhaps you have heard of the concept that it takes seven contacts on average, before a relationship becomes an ongoing relationship and a partnership. I attended my Alma Mater's Homecoming. It was fun connecting with past acquaintances and friends, and making new connections. Opportunities to gain, share, and give were abundant. While I sat in the plane back to San Francisco, I strategized about how to best follow up with the new and renewed contacts.

Top 5 Strategies to Successful Follow Up:

1. Integrity - Whatever path you choose to follow up, do it with integrity. Communicate with openness that is heartfelt and true to you. This is not the time to put on an act. Your approach best comes from a giving and kind space.

2. Timeliness - Communicate before you get home or to your office, or before you get back into your rut of daily to dos and activities. I make copious notes on business cards and agendas to remind myself what topics were discussed, and where I might be able to add value. My intention is to follow up with everyone at least via email.

3. Strategy - Ask yourself how you want to proceed with your contact. Maybe you want to invite her to one of your social networks, i.e. Linked-In, Facebook, DBCoach Club and so forth. Perhaps you want to send them an article about something you discussed. Why not make a follow up phone call to review some action items? Whatever your strategy, make it intentional.

4. Be Consistent - Remind yourself by entries in your calendar, on your to-do-list, or with reminders to your cell phone to stay on track. Don't drop the ball now! And don't forget to follow up on your follow up.

5. Pay It Forward - in a sense you have received the gift of a connection. This gift is an opportunity. Be generous with your giving in the relationship building process. One of our fellow T-Birds, whom I met years ago and stayed in contact with, was just diagnosed with Lou Gehrig's Disease. In addition to participating in several clinical trials, he will soon be traveling to Germany to have a stem cell transplant, a procedure not currently done in the US for this disease. Since his insurance doesn't cover the cost, many of us were happy to help out by donating to his very personal cause. You never know whether someday you might need support from others - so pay it forward! Without a doubt, even more can be done to manifest lasting relationships, but if you consistently engage in my list of 'Top 5,' your network will exponentially increase, and function as a valuable resource.

THE LAST 10%

"Opportunity is missed by most people because it is dressed
in overalls and looks like work."

~ Thomas Edison, *An Enemy Called Average*

How often do we miss opportunities because we don't put our full effort into reaching our goal? Like many of you, I watch the Olympic events on TV. While watching one of the swimming races I was fascinated by the seemingly effortless ease with which the athletes glide through the water. One doesn't recognize, until the close up of the athlete at the end of the race, how much effort was put into every second, in fact, every millisecond of the race. One event in particular sticks in my mind - the women's 200-yard breaststroke. The winner was in second place the entire 200 yards of the race, and yet, she won by 28/100th of a second.

One of my clients told me about his daughter's most recent swim meet. He was a designated timer for the event and observed many swimmers reaching the finish line. He was surprised at how many kids seemed to stop their efforts when they got close to the finish line. They were sort of coasting in, because they saw the wall, and mentally, were already finished. The winners, however, continued with full effort all the way to the end.

How many times have you heard of someone selling a home and then you find out that the sale fell out of escrow? Anyone in sales has come across this scenario. You feel as if you have sold the house, car, product, service, and idea. But unless the papers are signed and the money has transferred, the deal is not complete.

Often we feel so close, because we want it to happen so badly, but we can't quite get there. So, what's missing?

Either we stop our efforts right before the finish line - not conducive to being a winner. We think we are done when in fact we are not. Or, the final decision is actually out of our control. We cannot control other people's actions. We can anticipate certain actions, but we cannot make people do things. All we can do is trust our intuition that the parties involved are a good match at this moment in time. This last phase when the deal seems done, but actually isn't complete takes just as much energy as all the research and actions that took place before.

First, it's the physical work getting everything together, the paperwork, the interview, the testing, but then the process shifts to a mental exercise, where you can't do anything anymore, but you are thinking about it a lot. The wait seems endless and takes much energy out of us. We are really not done until the ink is dry. Then and only then is it time to move on.

Reflections:
What have you done to complete a deal, a real estate transaction, a sale, a raise, a promotion, and a new job opportunity? Is it really complete with the ink dry on the contract? Or are you heading towards the final stages?

If you have done your part, are you giving others a chance to do their part to complete the deal?

So what is incomplete for you? In my work with clients I am able to observe from the outside, if something is complete, and it often helps to reflect on where you are in the process. Until the deal is done, work with full energy towards the physical, and mental, work that is required to ensure that you pass the finish line a winner.

ARE YOU PLAYING THE BLAME GAME?

"If you don't accept responsibility for your own actions,
then you are forever chained to a position of defense."
~ Holly Lisle, *Fire in the Mist*

In her book *Secrets of the Six Figure Women*, Barbara Stanny wrote: *When a corporate culture is blatantly unhealthy, the best thing we can do is leave for someplace more supportive. And that's what many women I interviewed eventually did, the majority following a national trend, opting out of the corporate world altogether.*

Many executives find themselves unsatisfied at work and feel unsupported by their management. Managers all too often feel powerless. Often executives' expectations and goals don't match the goals, and objectives, of their management. People are looking for meaningful work, a way to make a difference; they want to improve processes, sales, change something for the better.

And yet executives are frustrated with their boss, mostly because they can't find an effective way to communicate with him. Managers feel a lack of control when it comes to their own career. Executives want to make a difference, but they don't seem to be allowed to run with their ideas - a sign of lack of clarity regarding goals and expectations. They want to learn, but requests for ongoing training are often denied.

Lack of appreciation, respect, and trust sabotage relationships at work. Sometimes this process goes on for years, leaving the employee struggling with self-esteem, self-worth, and self-confidence. The once motivated and dynamic employee begins a downward spiral, which often ends with the individual being laid-off or quitting.

Some of my clients come to me seeking help to get out of the spiral. Many have already resigned internally. They have started the blame game! It's everyone else's fault, the company, the boss, management, and the economy. Many of them are so demotivated, the only solution they can see is to quit, and they would have done so earlier, if not for the fear factor, the fear of not finding another job in a poor economy, and the fear of no income. Little do they realize that their boss is often in the same spiral.

My work starts with raising an individual's awareness. Let's face it, there will be a boss in the next work place, either above us or within us. It's time to learn how to be a satisfied/happy/fulfilled employee/ manager.

First and foremost - let's stop the blame game. It's not anybody else's fault we are in the situation we are in. We are a product of our own choices. Our choices are what got us here and our choices can get us out. So, rather than pointing fingers, let's choose to become aware:

1. Realize our right to make choices
We have a right to make choices, and so do our bosses. Allow her to look at options and make choices. Sometimes she makes decisions we don't understand. And yet she made the decision to the best of her ability given her set of information. If you don't understand why a decision was made, ask. You might get

a piece of information you weren't aware of. The same principle applies in reverse: Allow your employees the right to have choices and make decisions. There is no need to micromanage, if you trust your employee to do her best. It is our responsibility to support our employees, as well as our managers, to be the best they can be.

2. Realize the only constant is change

We all know the only constant is change, but most of us dread change, because we don't know what to expect. Yet, once on the other side, most people will say: *I wish I had made the change a long time ago.* My happiest clients are the ones who embrace change. Embracing change also means taking risks, calculated risks, risks that are challenging, and yet set them up for success. Baby steps work well!

3. Realize priorities

If you don't know what's most important to you, you can't ask for it. You risk having others guess what you want. If you don't want others to assume what's best for you, tell them. If you don't know what's most important to you, hire a coach to help you uncover what you want. Learn to ask what's most important to your boss. She might have completely different priorities than you thought. So, you spend hours finishing the report, when making client calls would have been more important to her. Check in regularly with your boss asking *what's most important to you*?

4. Realize the other person's needs

We all have wants, desires, needs. Let's find out what your boss needs. Does she need to be listened to or acknowledged?

Does she need to be respected or liked? In a sense it is our responsibility to make our boss look her best. How do we ever hope to accomplish this, if we aren't aware of her needs? And in reverse, how can we ever have a satisfied employee, when we aren't aware of what she needs, i.e. tools, support acknowledgment, encouragement.

Reflections:
"What would I want my ideal boss to be like?"
Think about it and then write it down.
Then ask yourself: "Am I the ideal boss?"

Most likely, your employees want those qualities from you as well.

WHAT DECISION ARE YOU STALLING ON?

"In a world where death is a hunter,
there is no time for regrets or doubts.
There is only time for decisions."
~ Carlos Castañeda, *Journey to Ixtlan*

Any decision is always better than no decision. Again, any decision is always better than no decision. You can always make a new decision. People hesitate to make decisions for fear of unintended outcomes. Hesitation and lack of decision making leads to stress and frustration. Not making decisions is costly, time consuming, and inefficient.

Let me give you a very personal example. I will remember 2008 as the year I didn't buy a car. Twice in January and in September, I walked into my local dealership; check in hand anticipating driving home in a new car. During the first meeting, we couldn't agree on the price. During the second meeting the car I wanted had been inadvertently sold from underneath me. I brushed it off thinking that I wasn't meant to have a new car in 2008. The whole car buying experience made me realize I don't like buying cars, not because I don't like cars, on the contrary. I don't like the whole experience of walking into a dealership and being *sold* to. Some people thrive on the shark environment (my Dad being one of them). I despise it. Strong word, I know, but I really don't like it.

Upon reflection, I decided maybe it was time to let go of the loyalty I had to that particular dealership. Maybe it wasn't all about me. I approached a second dealership. During the sales process, I was treated with courtesy and respect. I had been holding on to my loyalty instead of searching for what worked for me. In all fairness, it wasn't all about the dealership. Lots of variables changed in my car buying decision - dramatic changes in fuel prices, unexpectedly fewer children in my house, lots of discussions about environmentally friendly cars (I do live in California where this is even more of a topic), and of course the economic downturn. As a result, I have been *buying* a car for a year. I don't know how many hours I have researched cars on the Internet, looked at cars on the road and talked to people about their cars and their car purchasing experiences. It's just mind-boggling how much time, and energy, I have invested in this purchase. I am happy to report that by the time you read this, I will be the proud owner of a new vehicle (yes, I am doing my part to stimulate the economy).

Whatever you haven't made a decision on is robbing your energy. Not making a decision continues to hang over your head, in your personal and business life.

What decisions are you stalling on - hiring an employee, firing an employee, starting a business, closing a business, selling a business, buying versus renting? Whatever it is, make the decision and move on - time is too precious!

WORK SMARTER, NOT HARDER

"The key is not to prioritize what's on your schedule,

but to schedule your priorities."

~ Stephen R. Covey, *The Seven Habits of Highly Effective People*

Whether you are an executive, entrepreneur or a mom, all of us are challenged when trying to get a multitude of things done. There never seems to be enough time. We are adding more and more time saving devices, but the more gadgets we have, the less time we seem to have. Many people seem to think the answer is to multitask and get two, or even three, tasks done at the same time. They pride themselves in being great multi-taskers. However, multitasking is an illusion. Multitasking is actually rapid mental task switching. When we engage in multi-tasking, the quantity, and quality, of our work is degraded.

I believe we can work effectively by limiting the frequency of rapid task switching.

A rejection I often encounter, when discussing multitasking, is from people who are convinced they can do two things at once, i.e. talk with someone while opening their mail, or drinking coffee while checking their email, or making a phone call while the computer is booting up. I won't argue that we are all capable, but I know that with increasing complexity of each task, a higher level of concentration is required. Then interruptions, and distractions, must be minimized in order to produce quality results in an efficient manner.

Here are some strategies to work smarter:

Manage Expectations:
Too often we assume we know what is expected of us. Instead of assuming, we need to get clarity about others' expectations of us.

a) Identify Deadlines (Could this wait until next week?)
b) Clarify Specifications (What specifically are you looking for?)
c) Address Conflicts (If I work on project A then project B will be delayed.)
d) Specify Agreements (You'll have it on your desk tomorrow morning.)

Plan Effectively:
We tend to multitask more when we are running behind. Productivity, and quality, of our work goes down and leaves us feeling frazzled. Proactive planning allows us to stay ahead. Subsequently, emergencies can still be dealt with without missing deadlines.

Give yourself permission to say *no*. Saying *no* to tasks that are not important (those with few or no consequences) enables us to get the important tasks done well.

Work Efficiently:
Here are five strategies to improve efficiency and decrease the need to multitask:

1. External Memory
Don't try to keep lists in your head; instead write things down electronically or manually. Holding on to data limits our brain's capacity to solve complex problems. Keeping information in your memory unnecessarily also drains our energy.

2. Minimize paperwork
Properly stored electronic files are simple to search and can be retrieved easily. See if you can keep paper documentation to a minimum. If you are concerned about losing electronic files, upgrade your back up systems.

3. Use technology
Rather than deciding in favor of the newest gadget, decide in favor of reliability. Choose technology that is simple to integrate and works best for you.

4. Delegate
Ask yourself: Do I really need to do this? Who else can do this? Who can I train do to this in the future?

5. Focus on completion
Don't get frustrated by unfinished tasks. Break tasks down, if they don't fit into an allotted time frame. Plan in advance where you want to stop.

Reflections:
What is expected of me?
Who is expecting it?
When is it expected by?
What do I need to clarify about expectations?
What is happening within the next week, next month next year that I can plan ahead for now?
What do I need to write down that is on my mind constantly?
What can I delegate up, down, or sideways?

STOP TOLERATING YOUR HABITS

"Creativity can solve almost any problem. The creative act,
the defeat of habit by originality, overcomes everything."

~ George Lois, American art direction

Spend some time focusing your attention on self-awareness of your personal work style, and how you approach certain tasks.

1. Limit distractions, but add reminders (sights and sounds)
Depending on the office environment you work in, you can take certain steps to reduce the amount of distractions. If you work in a cubicle, or share an office with colleagues, reserve a conference room to get important projects done. Don't be afraid to close your office door from time to time, or turn the sound of your telephone off. On the other hand, introduce visual and auditory reminders, such as an alarm set for the time you have to leave the office, or dial into a conference call. Post-it notes, and other visual reminders, can help you focus on what's most important.

2. Determine the complexity of certain tasks
The more complex the task, the more you have to eliminate distractions. Simple tasks lend themselves more for multitasking. Keep in mind that completing more complex tasks will leave you more satisfied about your accomplishments.

3. Break simple tasks down into simple stand-alone operations.
Let's say one of your projects is to bring a product to market, potentially quite an overwhelming prospect. Breaking it down makes it manageable:

Step 1 – Proposal to management
Step 2 – Identify action committees, and so on. Even Step 1 could be broken down into a) researching the issues and b) writing the proposal.

4. Prioritize

Do the most important task first, not the task that is easiest to get accomplished. How do you gauge the importance of a task? The more severe the consequence of failure is, the more important the task. In other words tasks where, by not doing them or delaying them, the consequences are most harsh. My editor calls these "crying babies," tasks that cannot be ignored.

5. New Tasks

If you encounter a task that you haven't done before, you need to focus with undivided attention, until you have passed the learning curve. We all had to think about the details for driving a car when we first started driving. Now we don't even think about where the break, or gas pedal, is.

6. Lengthen your attention span

The shorter your attention span, the more you will be inclined to multitask. But you can train yourself to resist the urge to switch tasks until you come to a natural break in your work. Set natural milestones for yourself throughout the day.

7. Planning

Good planning eliminates stress and the last minute necessity to multi-task. A good plan always includes some contingency time, whether it's an extra 10 minutes to allow for unforeseen traffic, or 2 weeks before the actual product launch. If you work right up to the deadline without building in contingency time, unforeseen emergencies will jeopardize the project. Invariably an emergency will come up, so plan for it.

8. Work style
Are you naturally drawn to details? See if you can avoid becoming fixated on details. Focus on the bigger picture. Are you naturally drawn to ignore the details? Pay more attention to the details and focus on getting the task completed. Know your own work style.

9. Scheduling
Frequently, I will come across an individual who is struggling to fit in physical exercise or time for himself. My rule is simple: Schedule it or it won't happen. Why do we not have a problem scheduling meetings at work, but we struggle to schedule time to read a book or take a walk? Have the courage to schedule anything that is truly important to you.

10. Transition time
Allow yourself some transition time between tasks. Allow your mind to switch gears between tasks by getting up and walking around. I personally need 10 minutes of grounding time between talking with clients and picking up my kids.

Reflections:
Pick one of the ten factors described above, the one where you seem to struggle the most. Then stop tolerating it and see if you can change your habit.

SYSTEMS

"It is best to do things systematically, since we are only human,
and disorder is our worst enemy."

~ Hesiod, Greek poet

Time - all of us want more time. Time is a finite commodity. We seem to be running out of it all day long - in fact we are. There never seems to be enough time to do everything. Tax time is a perfect example. We know all year that the deadline is April 15, but the crunch comes at the end. Everybody has their own system for preparing taxes. The options run from receipts stuffed in a shoebox to automatically downloaded bank account information into a software program like Quicken or Money. Regardless of your choice of filling out the tax forms yourself, or having them prepared by a CPA, somehow you need to keep track of income and expenses. Because you need to keep track anyhow, you might as well automate the process as much as possible. Reducing the work into smaller chunks helps. You could set aside 2 hours a month to organize your tax information from the previous month. If you get into the habit of designating time to do tax information every month, then you don't have the pressure come March or April. Whether you are designating time monthly or prefer the rush in the end, here are some questions to ponder every time you are dealing with a recurring task:

What part of your 'system' needs improving?
You spend too much time shuffling through statements at tax time. You don't want to procrastinate until the end, so you must be proactive every month.

What resources do you need to improve your system?
For example, rather than just looking up information from filed statements you might want to invest in software to keep all the data for you.

How can you automate the process?
You might want to download your bank information into your computer automatically. You don't have to spend time keying in the information and you have instant access to your financial information.

What templates process can you create to help remind yourself?
You can block out 2 hours every month to dedicate to getting your financial house in order, i.e. pay and file bills, download bank information, create monthly reports.

Investing some time up front by improving and automating your systems continually, rather than the mad dash at the end, takes less time overall, and gives you peace of mind. Incidentally, improving your system applies to your household, your business, even your leisure time.

Reflections:
Do you have a system in place?
What can you do today to improve and automate your systems?

NEGOTIATING 101

"Let us never negotiate out of fear. But let us never fear to negotiate."

~ John F. Kennedy, *Inaugural Address*

Would you consider yourself a good negotiator? You don't think you need to be a good negotiator? Think again! All of us negotiate several times every single day! As a matter of fact, it pays to get really good at it. What are some of the things we may need to negotiate?

- A pay raise in your current position
- Salary for a new position
- Purchase or sale of real estate
- Rental fees for an apartment or a car
- Details of a business merger
- An exit strategy from an existing job
- Who is in charge of finances among couples
- Allowances
- Garage sale pricing

The list is endless. But I think you get the point. We are constantly negotiating. In order to get really good at negotiating, we must practice, practice, practice. My son and I are making a game of it. He is a natural negotiator and it is easy for him to get what he wants - he also makes a great sparring partner for me. He is teaching me how not be too attached to the outcome, while sticking to what I want. Here is my personal top ten list of do's and don'ts when it comes to negotiating:

1. Do your homework:
The more information you have the better. If you are interviewing for a job, get as much information as you can about the com-

pany, their salary ranges, salaries in the state/region/city, and so forth. Research, research, research. This works for many situations! Before my son negotiates for a new video game, he knows which games are out there, how much they cost, where to get them and what the benefits of each particular game are.

2. Let the adversary start the negotiation:
Why do you think interviewers always ask for a salary range before or during an interview? You are sort of locked in once you throw out a number.

3. Silence is golden:
Most people talk too much when they are negotiating. If you are silent, your adversary will feel inclined to fill the gap.

4. Avoid assumptions:
We often confuse assumptions with preparations. We try to consider what the other person is thinking or what the conditions are. In the process we make assumptions, so we don't really know what is going on. The easiest way to avoid making assumptions is by asking questions of the people we are interacting with to clarify.

5. Show vulnerability:
By opening yourself up and showing some vulnerability, your adversary might actually bail you out. It is a risk worth taking.

6. Ask for more:
Especially in high value negotiations, asking for more than you think you can get is a good strategy. It leaves room for compromise.

7. Know your options:

The more options you feel you have, the better negotiating position you are in. Ask friends, and family members, to help you explore all your options.

8. Be clear on your deal breaker:

What situation would make you walk away from the table? This is your worst-case scenario, and an important point to note for yourself. What amount would you still feel comfortable with, and what lower amount leaves you feeling taken advantage of?

9. Avoid being too willing to compromise:

Your adversary will generally sense your willingness to give in and take advantage of you. I can think of many examples where I have fallen into this trap. Awareness and assertiveness will help you stand firm!

10. Never need anything:

If you are too attached to the outcome and you are needy, your adversary can sense it. Don't enter into a negotiation unless you are willing to walk away from it.

Many books have been written about negotiating and many center on variations of my top ten. However, there is more to negotiating than knowing a number of tricks, even though tricks may help. Becoming a successful negotiator requires a certain state of being - high self-esteem, self-respect, self-assurance, intelligence, clarity, and being a good listener. Walk into the job interview, meet with your boss or your clients knowing that you are going to walk out of the meeting having negotiated your better position. The only way to become a great negotiator is to practice, practice, and practice.

Reflections:
Are you being too polite or fearful to negotiate a better position?
What have you negotiated today?
What better position can you find yourself in tomorrow?

EMAIL LIFESAVERS

"Words, once they are printed, have a life of their own."

~ Carol Burnett, American actress and comedian

Often my clients bring up the topic of email. On the one hand email can save tremendous amounts of time. On the other hand, email can also waste a lot of time and energy.

If you were to log your email usage, you would most likely be astounded to find how much time you spend on checking, responding to, writing, and managing your email.

Have you ever looked at the emails you sent in one day? If you can, do it now. How many of them were responses to requests from others - meaning *reactive*? And how many of them were emails you initiated to get something accomplished - meaning *pro-active*? Ideally you want to send a greater number of *pro-active* versus *reactive* email in order to feel a greater sense of accomplishment! I check this daily.

People ask me, how do you manage all your emails? Following are my personal guidelines on the effective use of email:

1. Decide in advance when to check email.

Checking email twice a day or at most three times a day is sufficient. Be disciplined about checking at 9:00 am and at 4:00 pm if those are the times that work for you. Some of my clients won't check their email until 10:00 am. They want to get something proactive done, before they react to other's requests.

2. Delete any spam or unwanted email without even opening it.

Once opened, you get sucked into the vortex of the subject. Before you know it, you click on a link and off you are surfing the web. Be careful not to get distracted from your primary goal for the day!

3. Create folders according to subject matter, i.e. clients, prospects, marketing, orders, family, and so forth.

Once you read an email, decide, if it requires action. If not, delete or file it. If it requires action, decide if you need to let the sender know you received the email and when you will be able to work on it.

4. Clean out folders on a regular basis.

Full folders will slow down your system and make it harder to search for what's really important.

5. Establish an email standard for yourself:

Anytime you send an email, you are communicating to someone else. Ask yourself how your message will be received:

a) Did I choose a subject, which makes it easy for the recipient to prioritize?
b) Did I use a greeting? It's simply polite.
c) Do I have more than one topic in my email? Maybe I need to split it into two emails to ease follow up.
d) Is my email requiring an action? If so, did I state my expectation in the first few lines, ideally including a due date?
e) Did I use the right address for the recipient?

f) Did I check my spelling/ grammar to portray professionalism and avoid misunderstandings?
g) Was I brief and to the point?

Establishing, and maintaining, an email standard enhances your communication, your professionalism, and helps avoid mistakes. Remember each email reflects on who you are and how you project yourself!

6. Acknowledge receipt of email.
If you can't act on a request right away, acknowledge receipt of the email, and state when you will get to it. It keeps the other party informed.

7. Save time and energy by not forwarding hoax email messages and chain letters.
They usually promise untold riches or ask for your support for a charitable cause. Even if the message seems to be legitimate the name of the sender is often forged.

8. Decide on urgency.
Is the matter urgent? You might be better off to pick up the phone and call to get an immediate response rather than send an email, where you have to wait for a reply.

THE NEED TO BE PERFECT

"Perfectionism is simply putting a limit on your future. When you have an idea of perfect in your mind, you open the door to constantly comparing what you have now with what you want. That type of self criticism is significantly deterring."

~ John Eliot, *Reverse Psychology for Success*

Some of you might be able to relate to this: I have been known to be a perfectionist at times. In my home, my car, my work, everything has to be just so. My expectations for myself have always been quite high. Does that sound familiar?

Having kids and increasing responsibilities in my personal and business life, I have learned to let go and get things done without dwelling too much about getting things just right.

Recently, I had a *light bulb* experience. At a digital storytelling workshop, I was faced with the challenge of writing a story, collecting, formatting, and importing a multitude of images, recording a voiceover, selecting a soundtrack, and finally editing everything into a cohesive, heartfelt and personal digital story. This task was to be done in only three days. Truthfully, I could have labored over every part for days.

In the workshop, we were given milestones. For example, the story had to be written by 5:00 pm on Day 1. The voiceover had to be recorded by noon the next day. The rough edit had to be done by 11:00 am the following day. In order to meet each target, I found myself struggling to find just the right sentence or researching just the right image, the perfect music or the best editing technique. However, the goal was to go home with a completed project – not perfect individual pieces.

By breaking it down in to smaller milestones, I made decisions along the way. Was it perfect? No. Was it the best I could do given the time? Absolutely!

On the last day, everything had to come together. I felt proud and the digital story had turned out much better than I had imagined. The individual pieces put together turned into a complete project.

Not only was I happy with the project, I was proud to have completed the project in a given time frame.

How was it possible? Here are the elements that worked for me: Prepare and plan. Don't start until you have all the necessary pieces ready to go.

- Focus on just one project. Don't allow any distractions from anybody or anything.
- Break down tasks with defined milestones.
- Have a vision of the end result.
- Have a coach to keep you on target.

I couldn't have done it on my own. Not only did I not have the necessary technical expertise, I would have most definitely stood in my own way trying to be a perfectionist.

I walked away with much more than the completed project. I walked away with light bulbs turned on.

MONEY

ARE YOU DRIVEN BY MONEY OR DRIVING IT?

"A wise man should have money in his head, but not in his heart."

~ Jonathan Swift, Irish novelist and essayist

We are living in a fearful world. When we are not concerned with life threatening natural disasters or where the next terrorist strike will hit, we are worried about money. Actually, we are almost obsessed with the fear of not having enough to begin with, or not making enough or running out altogether.

Fear of money is driving much of what we do every day. Some of us might continue to stay in our frustrating job, because it pays well or at least it pays the bills. Others avoid the subject of money and pretend it's just there, so they use their credit cards to the maximum. Others park it under the mattress - just in case. Then there are the investors jumping from one promising stock to the latest real estate deal ready to flip it fast for instant gratification.

What is it about money that makes us do things we really don't want to do, but we feel compelled to because we all need money to survive and, hopefully, maintain or upgrade our life style?

Have you ever examined your relationship with money? Do you view money as positive or negative, friend or foe? Those of you who view money negatively most likely grew up with beliefs, such as 'there isn't enough', 'we can't afford it' or 'it doesn't grow on trees.' Those of you who view money positively probably believe there is an abundance of money. It's just a matter of how it gets distributed.

If you have negative beliefs concerning money, you are most likely driven by money, i.e. you need your paycheck to pay your bills, you might have credit card debt, you are wondering where to get the money for the next tax payment.

If you have positive beliefs around money, you are most likely driving money. You are proactively setting up bill payments, you only have good debt, you have plenty in the bank to pay the next tax bill and you are actively searching out ways to reduce your tax bill to begin with. You know your net worth and you have a good handle on your cash flow. Which would you rather be, driven by money or driving money?

Reflections:
What will it take to be in the driver seat of your own money train?
What do you believe about money?
What changes can you make today to be in control of your financial situation?
What do you need to update/create your personal income statement and balance sheet?
Who can you align yourself with to learn how to manage your money better?

IMPACTING THE BOTTOM LINE

"He who labors diligently need never despair; for all things
are accomplished by diligence and labor."
~ Meander, Greek playwright

Why were you hired? Probably because you were the best candidate for the job. Time to feel proud of yourself? But wait. There might be another reason. Could you have been hired to make a positive contribution to the organization's success? What does that actually mean? Perhaps there was a problem your organization needed help with; the problem most likely still exists. Perhaps the organization didn't have enough, or the right kind, of people to get the problem solved. Unfortunately, you were hired and became an immediate liability. Why? Because even if you are really smart, you don't know the products and services well enough, you don't know the culture of the organization, and you don't know the political climate you were hired into. The company has made an investment in you. They need to train you to be productive, and more importantly, they need you to have a positive impact on the bottom line. They need to see a return on their investment. Otherwise you remain a liability and don't become an asset.

Here is my #1 tip for every employee around performance review time: Come prepared with a list of accomplishments that impacted the bottom line positively. Individuals rarely come prepared with this information. The list will make your performance appraisal more successful and can be used to update your resume in the future. It's the best guarantor for job security.

Reflections:

How have you impacted the bottom line this month? This year?

What accomplishments have you achieved that make you the best person for the job?

What changes can you make to ensure that when it's appraisal time you receive high praises and even a promotion?

WHAT IS YOUR RELATIONSHIP WITH MONEY?

"Money is the opposite of the weather. Nobody talks about it,
but everybody does something about it."
~ Rebecca Johnson, *Vogue*

After giving the topic of money much thought, I have come to the conclusion that people don't like to talk about money - at least not their own money. Money is sort of a taboo subject in our culture. Nobody wants to talk about how much money they make or how much money they have for various reasons: 1. You don't want to look like you are bragging, meaning you don't want to look too egotistical. 2. You don't want anyone to know that you are struggling to make ends meet.

Who do you talk to about your financial affairs? Your accountant? Your financial advisor? Your spouse? Your kids? Your parents? What is it about money that makes us so secretive about it? What are we afraid of that compels us to hold our financial cards very close to our chests?

A friend recently told me a story in which one child tells her friend that the horse her parents bought cost $5,000. My friend pointed out that adults most likely wouldn't have mentioned the actual cost of the horse. Obviously the children didn't think twice about it. Adults seem to treat money as a taboo subject. What makes it so difficult to ask for money: for a raise, in exchange for our products and services, for advice on how to best manage our money?

I believe the issue around money comes down to three things:
   1. Clarity   2. Courage   3. Detachment from outcomes.

1) First we need to know what we want money for. What are we seeking? How much do we need and want? Knowing what we want is important, but we also need the courage to ask for it.
2) How many employees don't get a raise, because they don't have the courage to ask for it? I bet the number is staggering. So, go ahead and ask for what you want.
3) The third thing is detaching yourself from the outcome. If an employer or a potential investor in your business says *no*, what is she really saying *no* to? You personally? Most likely not. Most likely the *no* comes from the circumstances, for example the fact that she doesn't have more money in the budget. Let's face it, she would most likely much prefer to say *yes* than *no*, don't you think?

Reflections:
What is your relationship with money?
What is unclear about your financial situation?
Who can you ask and what will it take to ask?
What will it take to not take it personally?

WHAT PROFIT MARGIN HAVE YOU SET?

"There are always opportunities through which businessmen can profit
handsomely if they will only recognize and seize them."
~ J. Paul Getty, American Industrialist

Running your own business is scary. Not everyone is cut out for
the potential roller coaster ride that awaits every entrepreneur.
Not knowing what next month's income looks like is cause for
many sleepless nights.

We have all heard the notion of paying yourself first. Easier
said than done when you are just starting out and you don't
know if you will be able to sell your product or service. I have
had my business for 10 years now and it hasn't always been
easy. There were certain months I didn't pay myself at all, but
then other months made up for it. I have learned how to live
with uncertainty and can't even imagine what it would be like
to get a steady paycheck. But even if you are one of the ones
with a steady paycheck, uncertainty might creep into your personal finance picture. Children, a home, health concerns, and
so forth add to the uncertainty. How do I manage financial
stress? I shoot for a 25% profit margin. Everything I embark
on, my business, my personal finances need to generate 25%
more income than expenses. It looks simple but it's not. I make
it part of every goal I strive for, and it has become ingrained. I
don't always achieve this goal. No I don't. But without this goal,
I never even come close.

Reflections:
What profit margin do you want to set for yourself?
What changes will you make to make to get there?

WHO ARE THE MEMBERS OF YOUR MONEY TEAM?

"None of us is as smart as all of us."

~ Ken Blanchard

I don't know – do you? I admit it, I don't have the answers most of the time, especially when it comes to finances and money (actually that statement applies to a great many things). I only know very little about money. But I know where and how to get the answer.

Growing up I thought I needed to find a bank and maybe establish a relationship with a banker. By now, I have a whole team of people I can count on when needed: a bookkeeper, a certified public accountant, a lawyer, a banker, a mortgage broker, a property manager, a financial advisor, a financial planner. If dealing in more than one business or country, you might need several of these experts. At the end of the day all of these people will provide you with information. And yet they are looking to you to make the decisions. This is where my little bit of knowledge comes in. I know enough to dissect a balance sheet and an income statement and I know where I want to go financially. Plus I have a set of standards or principles that I will adhere to. All these experts help me figure out how to get there. It's that simple. Actually, it's not that simple. But with a team of trusted advisors, I feel I am moving the ship in the right direction and I am making progress. Do I get it right? Hopefully, more often than not. Do I make mistakes? Yes, but as long as I learn from the lessons, I am all right with it. Having a trusted team helps me minimize those mistakes. It helps me to take calculated risks.

Reflections:

Who is on your financial team?

Are they helping get you to where you want and realistically can be?

Are you in need of a new member of the team?

Do you need to let a member of your financial team go?

HOW DO YOU HANDLE THE TAX SEASON?

"Money is a powerful aphrodisiac. But flowers work almost as well."

~ Robert Heinlein, American writer

Benjamin Franklin said: "Of two things you can be certain: Death and Taxes." There is not a whole lot we can do about death. We have a 100% success rate there. Taxes are certain as well, but at least we can affect the amount and the process to a certain extent. How can we affect the amount you ask? Well, you can't affect the going tax rate in your country, but you can affect how much income you generate, which in turn has an impact on how much you pay in taxes. People complain about taxes and tax increases. What they tend to forget is that only when one earns money does one pay taxes (property taxes are ignored for the time being). The more you earn, the more you have to pay. Anyone up for a lesser paying job so your tax bill is lower? Probably not. Yet there is a direct correlation between the taxes you pay and the income produced by YOU! So, you really are in control of the taxes you are paying.

Now, let's talk about the process. What does it take to: 1) file your tax return every year and 2) have the money available when you need it? To ease the process of filing, it takes organization. The same is true for having the money available. My motto is – take it one step at a time. I organize my income and expenses monthly with the help of the software program, Quicken. By the time taxes are due, I hand my Quicken income statement print-out to my CPA to finish the actual return. Painless! I automatically transfer a certain amount of money from my checking account to a savings account every month to take care of the upcoming tax bill. In a sense I force myself to automatically save. Baby steps get me there every time, and it's relatively painless. There is an initial investment of setting up the process, but after that it's smooth sailing. This might sound like a simplified process, but it applies to your personal finances just as much as your small business or a corporation. The principles are the same.

CUT YOUR SPENDING

"Perfection is achieved, not when there is nothing more to add, but when there is nothing left to take away."

~ Antoine de Saint-Exupery, French poet

Not that I am striving for absolute perfection, but moving in that direction might not be such a bad idea. With that in mind, six months ago, I focused on my expenses. All of my expenses and income are accounted for in Quicken, a financial computer program. There are other programs out there as well, i.e. QuickBooks, or Mint.com. Looking at all of the expenses, I created a list entitled: Potential Costs to cut. The list included reduced monthly telephone cost by 10% for the recirculation pump, or sell new tile sitting in the garage. Other ideas were using frequent flier miles for the next two trips and spending x amount less for groceries. My children came up with the idea of putting an egg timer in the shower to keep the showers to less than 5 minutes. A shorter shower left my children clean and saved me money. What I realized was that I could make minor adjustments without making an impact on my lifestyle. Sometimes these adjustments were huge and still didn't have much impact. I just needed to be aware and take action.

Reflections:

What do you need to be aware of when it comes to your expenses?

Where can you take away without suffering?

HAVE YOU FINISHED IT PROPERLY?

"Measure not the work until the day's out and the labor done."

~ Elizabeth Barrett Browning, English poet

"Finish things properly" is a phrase I heard Maria Shriver, California's First Lady, quote from her mother Eunice Shriver. That phrase keeps coming back to me. I often use similar expressions, such as *find completion* or *get closure*, in my own situations, as well as my clients'. It is a phrase that can be applied to every aspect of our lives, whether it is family, work, or money.

In these financially difficult times, I want to talk about the phrase *finish things properly* with regards to money. Building a house on an unstable foundation is not sound construction. We all know that. Likewise, we need a solid financial foundation to build our financial wealth on. All too often I come across people who have unfinished business, and yet they wonder why they are struggling to stand upright on their faulty foundation. Some of these individuals might not have their will completed, or a loan paid off, a divorce finalized, or have a business partnership hanging in the air. Being in any of these situations may lead to trouble in the future.

Not only is it difficult to build on this unfinished business, it is also energy draining – and stress inducing. What causes us to not complete something? By not closing, we keep things in the status quo, the known. The situation might be miserable, but at least we know what we have. Making the last bit of effort to close will bring change. Change is scary. We can't foresee the end results – it's unknown and unfamiliar – so we avoid it.

I made a conscious decision to close certain financial matters this year. I refinanced my house and paid off a car loan. I finished several financial conversations with business partners and clients. It feels good to close the year with finished business.

Reflections:

What unfinished business do you need to tackle?

What options do you have to complete financial transactions?

Who do you need to talk to in order to find closure?

WORKING TOGETHER FOR SUCCESS

"Your most precious possession is not your financial assets. Your most precious possession is the people you have working there, and what they carry around in their heads, and their ability to work together."

~ Robert Reich, American political economist

Years ago, I remember asking a local artist and business owner, Annie Morhauser, of Annieglass, at what point had her business become a success. Annieglass is a line of glass tableware that started in a small workshop in Watsonville, California. The small venture grew to a multimillion-dollar business supplying goods to Saks Fifth Avenue, Neiman Marcus and even the White House. Annie said her business took off the moment she established a good working relationship with a bank. She needed to borrow a large sum of money to move her operations to a bigger warehouse. Her relationship with her banker became a turning point in her business.

Bookkeepers, Accountants, Controllers, and CFOs are crucial players on a successful financial team. Everyone, and every business, needs access to financial advisers who put things in place so that their money works for them. And everyone needs advisors who can assess where money is wasted, and where expenses can be cut. We live in a complex financial world. If we have learned anything in this great recession, it is that we need to be the CEO of our own money team. We can't rely on one person to give us advice or know the answer. It takes a team. Who is on your money team?

ARE YOU FINANCIALLY LITERATE?

"Making money is art and working is art and good business
is the best art of all."

~ Andy Warhol, American artist

When I was working in the Kodak European Region Office, during a performance appraisal I was made aware of one of my shortcomings. I had built my career on the marketing side of the business. My boss told me that I really didn't have a financial background to make me eligible for certain positions in the organization. He was right. Despite having had accounting and finance classes in college and graduate school, I had never been interested in that side of the business. I radically changed that in the last 10 years. I have bought and sold residential and commercial real estate, I am managing portfolio investment, and I am in charge of my business finances covering income, expenses, and tax decisions. I am dealing with venture capitalists and loan officers in two countries. I deal with exchange rate fluctuations and rising and falling interest rates, profit and loss statements, income statements and balance sheets. It's a complex game of chess. Am I am going to be a financial expert tapped into the New York, London or Tokyo financial markets? Most likely not, nor do I want to be. But I have become financially literate. I understand the difference between good debt and bad debt. I have learned to interact with my financial team from a place of strength. They advise me, but I make the final decisions based on my vision and goals.

What about you? Are you financially literate? What will it take for you to be in control of your financial well-being? And who do you need to be to get there?

ARE YOU A DONOR?

"The excellence of a gift lies in its appropriateness rather than in its value."

~ Charles Dudley Warner, American essayist

Often, I find the terms *fundraising* and *development* in regards to philanthropy used interchangeably. In the dictionary you might find fundraising described as "the organized activity of raising funds." And development might be described as "the act, process, or result of developing." To me, development is relationship building and creating strategic alliances. On the other hand, fundraising covers events like auctions, walk-a-thons and festivals where funds are actively sought. Many non-profits focus, and spend, much of their energy on fundraising with many hours of labor spent organizing and setting things up. Often the more strategic work of developing and nurturing key donors and attracting significant grants is neglected. When was the last time you were been courted as a significant donor by an organization you support significantly? You might object by pointing out that we are in difficult times. Yes, that's true, but I find that especially in times of hardship people will give where it matters most. What do you think?

RANDOM ACTS OF KINDNESS

"The end result of kindness is that it draws people to you."

~ Anita Roddick, *A Revolution in Kindness*

Studies show that random acts of kindness have a positive effect on their giver. Upon reading that, I decided to give more. In these tough economic times, when resources are stretched so thin, acts of kindness are all that we can give. I started out with acts as small as holding the door open for someone or smiling at a stranger. Sometimes my actions went unnoticed, but I realized that it did not hinder my desire to continue. In helping strangers, however small the gesture, it made me feel better.

Next, I tried out my new philosophy on my family and my friends. I cooked my son his favorite meal – Schweinebraten – and had it waiting when he got home. I invited my friends over for dinner parties and treated them to good food that I knew they would enjoy. In German, the saying goes: Liebe geht durch den Magen. You can get to their heart through their stomachs. Seeing my family and friends sitting around my dining room table, enjoying their meal and the company around them, I recognized that my random act of kindness was as beneficial to me as it was to my guests.

Then I decided to up the ante. I decided to send each of my clients a letter and a check for $20 in the mail. They would not be aware they were going to receive it, or why. The results were amazing. Here are some of the letters that I received from my clients:

Hi Dany,

I have been behind on opening my mail. Last week, I opened your nice letter and check. How generous of you! Thank you so much, that is such a thoughtful and classy thing to do.

Kim

And then there was Kelly's note:

Hi Dany,

Thank you *so much for the $20 check - I don't know how to express it, but it is so kind of you. And, it also inspires me to think of how I can give back to everyone in my circle as well. I am so lucky to be your client and the time and money that I invest has been the greatest investment I have ever made, so thank you! I'm going to put the money toward the new pair of hiking shoes I've been wanting. Thank you!!! You are amazing.*

Always,
Kelly

My random acts of kindness brought so much to so many people. It didn't cost me much and yet, I received so much more in return. From the moment I conceived the idea to send money to my clients, to mailing the letters and checks, to receiving such gracious letters of thanks, I was rewarded again and again. And what makes it even better is hearing that my acts of kindness have influenced others to perform their own acts of kindness. They are paying it forward – something large grew from my small idea.

So what about you? How can you reach out to someone who isn't asking and make a difference in his or her life?

Take a moment to thank a family member, a friend, a colleague, a parent or a stranger. It doesn't take much, a friendly word, a note, an email, a phone call. Whoever is on your mind, touch base with him or her now. Don't let this moment pass and don't let another distraction take over.

Better yet, make it a habit. Why not give thanks to another person every single day this week?

HOW DO YOU CALCULATE YOUR CAPITAL?

*"The real measure of your wealth is how much you'd be worth
if you lost all your money."*
~ Unknown

What is capital? A dictionary definition reads: *The assets of a business that remain after its debts and other liabilities are paid or deducted.* Capital is often how wealth is defined, especially in regards to what is in the bank account. That is why people without money are perceived to be poor. But is that really true? Not necessarily.

I have met some very poor people who live very rich lives, when not viewed from a financial, capitalistic point. They might have very close family relations that are profoundly meaningful or impactful. Or they might be the sole keeper of the key to solving the crisis of mother earth. Some people define success by what they create. They might be starving artists, but their creations are immeasurably rich. Yet others define their success by the relationships they have made. Their riches are weighed by whom they know. Yet another group defines success by the credentials they have accumulated. The more three-letter acronyms that stand behind their name, the higher they consider their stock.

What value is there in being a self-made millionaire, when there is no creativity in your life or when your health is failing? Don't we need to take everything into account? Our financial well-being, our relationships, the environment we are creating, and our health - shouldn't our investment in all of these areas count for something? I think it does. I believe our success is defined by the human capital we have - the sum of all our parts. The digits on your bank slip do not hold more value than your ecological footprint. The pages of your family photo album are as valuable as the pages of your stock portfolio.

So, measure your own net worth. Calculate your capital – not just by adding up the numerical values. Examine the aspects of your life that provide you with pleasure and pride. Your relationships with your family and friends, your healthy body and mind, your involvement in the community, your dedication to our planet, your occupational and educational accomplishments – all these factors make you far richer than you may think.

ARE YOU FINANCIALLY DISCIPLINED?

"Success in business requires training and discipline and hard work.
But if you're not frightened by these things, the opportunities
are just as great today as they ever were."
~ David Rockefeller, American businessman

One of the definitions of discipline is a system of rules of conduct or method of practice. Discipline can come in many forms – from exercise and diet – to work ethic and education. I recently heard Marshall Goldsmith, author and executive coach for many CEOs, discuss self-discipline. We all need it -- no matter our job title or responsibilities. It is easy to think about controlling yourself in the work place. But the task becomes more difficult when we turn to financial discipline, the method of practice about how to handle one's money. Wealth sometimes comes in large windfalls, but more often than not, wealth is accumulated through hard work, careful planning, and discipline. Remember that starting simply and creating a habit that you can follow can lead to great results and great wealth.

The first step is to create a budget. Assess how your money must be allocated each month for bills. Mortgage, loan, credit card and car payments should be paid monthly, no matter how small the amount. Every dollar helps to get you owing less.

Also, take a good look at your other expenses. Where does your money go? Sporting events, clothes, dining out? Try to spend less on groceries, entertainment, or gas. By cutting down on extravagant spending, you can save more and spend it on the memories that will make a difference.

Though money may be tight, especially in these difficult financial times, try to take a small amount of your paycheck and put it in a saving account each month. It may be difficult to get into the habit and you may feel that you have to sacrifice, just to have money sit in the bank, but it will be worthwhile in the end. The more you accrue in your account, the more secure you will feel over time. Knowing that you have a security blanket waiting for you on that rainy day is worth the initial hardship.

Reflections:
Take a look at your finances.
Are you financially disciplined?
Are there steps that you can take to exert control over your money and over your future?
Are there areas in which you can cut back spending and save money?
Are you willing to take your budgeting from a once-in-awhile activity to a regular habit?

CREATING A FINANCIALLY SECURE TOMORROW

"A big part of financial freedom is having your heart and mind
free from worry about the what-ifs of life."

~ Suze Orman, American economist

There are those people who have a natural knack for money. They take a dollar and make it ten. And then there are the rest of us. Most of us are not born with economic instincts; our talents lie in other areas, and learning to deal with finances comes slowly and we make a few mistakes along the way.

The truth is that I had to learn about money the hard way. Throughout my marriage, I did not pay much attention to the finances and allowed my husband to take control of the money. I felt secure and safe, never thinking that my situation would change. It was only when I got divorced and was forced to stand on my own two feet that I began to consider my situation. It took some time, and I made a few missteps, but in time I learned to handle accounting, balance a checkbook, invest wisely, and set up a will and trusts. I am now the CEO and CFO of my household.

Why do I mention this? I have met many women who felt safe and secure in their marriages, just as I did. When their marriages failed, they felt hopeless and ill equipped to face their new financial situation. But as dire as their situations seemed, as humans they all were born with the ability to adapt to their new surroundings. Many of these women were not only able to learn to control their finances; they found that they enjoyed it! Managing money not only enables you to feel in control of today, it also provides you with security for tomorrow.

Reflections:

What is your current relationship with your finances?

Are there areas in which you can begin to manage and organize your money?

Before you find yourself in a situation where you feel helpless and ill equipped, empower yourself and become financially literate. Find some trusted advisors and map out your financial tomorrow.

WHERE IN YOUR LIFE ARE YOU EXPERIENCING ABUNDANCE?

"True abundance has nothing to do with anything I am HAVING, and everything to do with what I am BEING. When I share my abundance of beingness abundantly with all those whose lives I touch, everything I sought to have comes to me automatically, without my even trying to have them."
~ Neale Donald Walsch, American author

An article in the local newspaper caught my eye. The local lottery jackpot hit $183 million and kept growing. The newspaper article featured a local business owner, who had collected $20 each from ten employees, in his business, for a workplace lottery pool and subsequently purchased 200 tickets. The following quote sparked my interest in writing about the notion of abundance: "If we won it, we'd all split up the money, close the shop and we'd be doing something else." (Bobby Scott)

Two things come to mind: None of the people in this business seemed to be passionate about their work - very sad! Also, they were seeking abundance by gaining material wealth.

Whether you have ever bought a lottery ticket in your life or not, I am sure you have thought about what you would do with the money, if you won. Maybe you would pay down all your debt and the debt of everyone you love. Or you would travel around the world, or much like the business owner above, close down the shop and do something else. Your future would be secure, life would be perfect. Am I close?

What makes your life not perfect now? Why is it we never *have enough* of what we are looking for: money, time, love? We live in a state of not having enough. And yet, we all have abundance in our lives. The Merriam-Webster's Collegiate Dictionary defines abundance as: 1) an ample quantity: profusion, 2) affluence, wealth, 3) relative degree of plentifulness. I like the definition of an ample quantity: profusion, because it means we can experience abundance in ways other than material wealth.

I have realized that I am already abundant in so many other things in my life other than material wealth. I am abundant in my care about others. I am abundant in the amount of fun I am experiencing. I am abundant in many skills, such as communications and writing. I am abundant in my creativity and my spirit. I am abundant in love - the love I receive from family and friends as well as the love I have within myself that I share with others. The quote at the beginning of this anecdote sums it up nicely.

By not worrying about how to get things or how to pay the bills each month, but rather sharing our abundance with others, everything else falls effortlessly into place. The more you give with a full heart, the more you will receive. What an incredibly powerful thought! Does it work? Why don't you try it and see what happens?

Reflections:
Where are you experiencing abundance in your life, right now?
What do YOU have in abundance that you can give abundantly to others?
Look for three things you already have in abundance. For each one of these three things look for three ways you can share your abundance with others in the next 30 days. Then stand back and watch what happens!

DEBT CRISIS

"The Chinese use two brush strokes to write the word 'crisis.'
One brush stroke stands for danger; the other for opportunity.
In a crisis, be aware of the danger - but recognize the opportunity."
~ John F. Kennedy, American President

The United States is having a debt problem. The news about trillions of dollars that our children and grandchildren will have to pay off is disturbing. The news about European countries having to bail each other out is equally unsettling. Most of us don't have a direct impact on how government deals with debt problems, except with our votes. Instead of focusing on the Government, and how and what it should do, I want to focus your attention on your own issues and what you can do about them. First of all, I believe everyone can relate to the debt conversation. Regardless of how much or how little money any one of us has, we all have debt. Some of it is good debt; some of it is bad debt.

I consider good debt to be the debt you could pay off easily, if need be. The only reason you have this debt, is to make your cash flow situation easier, meaning it's easier to pay your regular bills. Also, Government often helps you to have good debt with write off incentives and tax credits. Why does the Government want you to have good debt? Good debt helps keep the economy going.

Bad debt is something you need to watch out for. Bad debt is the debt you get into, because you can't pay for what you are purchasing, even if you were to rearrange investments or sell a home. Bad debt is what is causing all the home foreclosures.

And bad debt strangles consumers, when they find they can only pay the minimum balance each month.

My rule of thumb is easy: Never accrue more debt than you can pay off, if you were to sell all of your assets, i.e. investments, home, car and so forth. This might be really conservative in some people's view. But it helps me sleep well at night. Once a year (at least), I list all of my assets and my liabilities. If my assets are worth more than my liabilities, I consider myself in good shape.

Like most people, I am subject to temptations in stores, in restaurants, when deciding to travel, and increasingly, on the Internet. One question I always ask myself before every purchase: Do I need this item or do I want this item? If I need an item, I ask myself, what need I am fulfilling with this purchase. Do I simply want an item? Is this purchase for pleasure? For fun? For others? *Want* items I always offset with spending cuts somewhere else.

When you can balance between your *want* and *need* items, you are already on the road to alleviating your debt.

Reflections:
What do you need this item for?
What do you want this item for?
Who do you want it for?
How will you pay for it?

GETTING OUT OF DEBT

"The significant problems we face cannot be solved at the same level of
thinking we were at when we created them"

~ Albert Einstein, German physicist

Once you have determined that you have bad debt and you want to get out from underneath it, you need to be willing to change your thinking. As we have all experienced in one way or another, changing our thinking is difficult to do. We are held tight by the thinking that got us into debt. The same reasoning that made us think it was ok to purchase xyz, makes us justify our actions by thinking—Everyone has debt, so why not me?

The main reason to eliminate debt is stress. Being in bad debt is a huge stressor that will eventually make you sick. I have been asked many times how to get out from bad debt therefore, I decided to include my list of top five ground rules that not only get you out of debt, but help you maintain a healthy debt level.

Before you dive in, list for yourself the pros and cons of getting out of debt. If you can list more pros than cons, you are ready to start:

1. Be aware

Know where your money is. This sounds simple, but many people, even high-level executives don't know where their money is and exactly how much they have. You might think this is impossible. I am telling you after coaching people at many different levels and all walks of life: It's true. Just because someone is driving a fancy car doesn't mean they don't have any bad debt. And it doesn't mean that they don't have financial worries.

At least once a year, do a financial physical on yourself. Create a Balance Sheet, listing your assets and liabilities. Include an income statement, listing your income and expenses. If you keep all your records on paper, write it down. If you are using online banking, download all of your activities with programs such as Quicken, Quickbooks or go to www.mint.com. Technology is so advanced now, there is no excuse to not be aware. Getting this financial snapshot is well worth the time it takes to put it together. I have never heard anyone not feel better after going through this exercise. Email me at db@dbcoach.com, if you want me to send you the balance sheet and income statement forms, I use, for free.

2. Pay off credit cards first
If you aren't paying your credit card off every month in full, start by increasing your payments to your credit card companies. Financial institutions are there not only to hold your money. They are pretty good at making money too. I believe I could live well on all the fees I am paying various vendors! Recent changes in reporting laws mandate that credit card companies state directly on the bill how long it will take to pay off the bill, if you only pay a minimum. Looking at those numbers makes me wonder, will people still be alive to pay off those bills? If you have trouble disciplining yourself, use debit cards, because they force you to have enough money in the account to cover what you are charging.

3. Spending less
Once you have your income statement, take a look at your expenses. Do you see any patterns? How much are you spending on groceries? How much on eating out? What about the

phone bill/s? Ask friends and family members how much they are spending on those same items. You might be surprised about some of the ideas people in your inner circle have about cutting costs. These conversations can be priceless. You are sitting on a goldmine of resources to cut your spending. Often I find, people are too ashamed to ask how others are able to cut expenses. Or they don't want to appear as being too nosy. You can always frame questions in a way that keeps them generic, i.e. how much money is reasonable to spend on groceries/month? Don't be shy. Come up with three action steps to reduce your spending!

4. Create More Income

You might think, easier said than done! True, creating income is not easy, but absolutely doable. It takes creativity and a willingness to be rejected. I can't tell you how many people are simply too afraid to ask for a raise, a different job, help to learn a new skill, and more. The times where people had one job, and that one job would satisfy their needs for their entire working life, are over. All of us need to be in the business of generating more income. Be creative. Ask your peers, friends, and family members what ideas they have. You might be surprised what they are doing. Come up with three action steps to create more income.

5. Saving Money

Now that you have lowered your expenses, and increased your income, it's time to save for hard times. A good number to shoot for is between 10% and 30% of your income. Many people say to me, I'll wait to see what's left over at the end of the month. That's not saving, that's wishful thinking. Set your checking account up, so a specific amount of your income is automatically placed into a savings account of some sort every month. Out of sight, out of mind. You'll be surprised how you can make do with the lesser amount in your regular account. Establish a goal or a dream that resembles what you are saving for, i.e. your children's college education, a house, and retirement. Having the money in your bank account when you need it takes the stress out of money matters. My children's dad and I started putting money away for our children's college education when they were born. Every year we each put a chunk of money to the side. It meant we had to be frugal in other areas, but we made it a priority. With the help of grandparents' additional contributions, now that they are ready to leave the nest, we don't have to worry about paying for our children's higher education. The money in the college fund has been set aside for a long time and has accrued compounded interest during that time. Planning ahead enabled us to avoid going into debt when it came time to send our children to school. I am no financial expert or mathematical wonder. All it took for me to get out of, and avoid, bad debt was to take the time to confront my spending and my future expenses. There's no reason why you can't do the same.

Reflections:
Are you aware of your spending?
Are you trying to spend less?
Are you working towards paying your credit cards off first?
Can you find ways to generate more income?
Take a moment to come up with three action steps to save more money.

IMPACT ON YOUR HEALTH

"We should manage our fortunes as we do our health - enjoy it when good, be patient when it is bad, and never apply violent remedies except in an extreme necessity."

~ Francois de La Rochefoucauld, French author

Money, work, and the economy top Americans' list of stressors, according to a survey on stress released (Nov. 9, 2010) by the American Psychological Association. Specifically 76% of Americans report money as a significant stressor. Stress in small doses isn't bad, because it helps you perform under pressure. Stress is a normal physical response to danger, causing a *fight or flight* reaction. Chronic stress, however, can lead to serious health problems.

Being a single-mom, entrepreneur, and homeowner, I feel I know a thing or two about dealing with stress caused by money issues. The stress level goes up when demands by the children increase as they grow up. The stress level is lower, when they act responsibly with the money they are given, or when they make some money. The stress level increases, when a client moves on, and it goes down when a new client signs up. Equally, the stress level rises when the property tax bill is due in November. But then I feel better when I see, at the year-end, that I have paid off x amount of my mortgage. I could cite many more examples. What I want to point out, however, is the fact that money issues are cyclical, much like a roller coaster ride. Sometimes you are on a high and sometimes you are on a low. When you are on a high everything seems to fall into place in regards to your financial well-being. When you are on a low, you seem to attract money problems like a magnet.

What I found important to remember is that my low and high feelings are just a response to the current state – a snapshot of good or bad. When I feel low I find looking at my income statement, and balance sheet help's me to get perspective. When I worry too much about money, I create even more money worries. More money worries create more stress. More stress on an ongoing basis, makes me sick, physically and emotionally. I find the worst part is abdicating control. We tend to think we can't do anything. We can't force finding a new job, we can't force a client to pay us up front, we can't force any flow of money. The more we force it, and are lacking control, the less money shows up. Our obesity epidemic, and our healthcare crisis, is partly the result of the money concerns of a majority of the population. Wouldn't it be nice if we could make money in our sleep? You might think this is funny, but some people do. What would it take for you to do the same?

FINANCIAL ANXIETY

"The more you chase money, the harder it is to catch it."

~ Mike Tatum, *Cashing In or Selling Out*

Are you worried about not having enough money?

The more you think of not having enough money, the more you will not have enough money. After reading the *Think and Grow Rich* by Napoleon Hill, I decided to focus on having enough and forget my anxieties that I may not have enough. Years ago, I committed myself to writing morning pages every day. Journaling helps keep my thoughts in check. Often, while writing in my journal, I solve (or resolve) an issue I have been grappling with. I decided to create one page, about three inches wide, that I use as a bookmark in my journal:

1. A poem or quote that inspires me (mine is in front of this book).
2. A picture of myself that I really like, where I look alive and happy and as if I could conquer the world.
3. Three goals that I absolutely want to achieve. One of them has to be money related and ideally it is a production goal rather than an outcome goal. For example, I want to work every day on creating more passive income, rather than I want to have a million dollars in a bank account.
4. State a reward for achieving those three goals, i.e. flying to Australia or having a party or something similar.

When I first started this, I wasn't convinced it would work. But I read my one-pager bookmark every day, when I was doing my journal entry. I focused on what I wanted to accomplish and saw myself accomplishing it. I have had incredible results with this process. It combines what I am encouraging my clients to do: journal writing, visualizing, setting goals, and being focused. This book couldn't have been written without this exercise.

Reflections:
What are you waiting for?
What is your focus?
What are you visualizing?
How are you conquering your financial anxiety?
Consider having your own journal to help you map out your
   feelings about money and alleviate your financial anxiety.

PURCHASING 101

"Fortune favors the brave."

~ Virgil, *Aeneid*

Buying seems easy. You go to the store and you pick out what you want, you then go to the cashier and pay, often with a plastic card. We accept the price marked on the item, and if we charge it to our credit card, we accept the fact that we have to pay it off. Something I have learned recently is that everything is negotiable. Everything! Because she will play Cinderella in *Into the Woods* next month, my daughter and I went to purchase a white dress, much like a wedding dress, to be modified into a Cinderella costume. If you have ever shopped for wedding dresses, you'll know that a) this is a laborious task and b) an expensive endeavor. Needless to say, neither one of us was really looking forward to the excursion. However, it needed to be done, so we met at the mall and discussed a plan of attack. We discussed the possibility of finding used wedding dresses, cocktail dresses at second-hand shops and thrift stores. Honestly, we were a bit at a loss. At one point I said: " Let's just walk in to Macy's right here and see what they have." I guess it was my way of taking some action rather than just discussing options. We found the department with evening gowns filled with a sea of blue and black dresses, long, short, fancy and sparkly. Tucked in the corner was one rack with 5 dresses, 4 beige ones of the same styles, not quite what we had in mind, and one white one. It was a sleeveless, long flowing dress. The chance this one dress would fit was really slim, so we kept looking, but couldn't find white dresses anywhere else. So my daughter decided to try the dress from Macy's on. We checked with a cashier about the price first, because the price tag had been ripped off. The cashier found the dress in the computer, and it had been marked down. Because it was the last white dress in the store, and it was reasonably priced, we decided to see if it would fit. It fit perfectly. My daughter looked lovely, and any alterations needed to make it look more 'Cinderella-y' could easily be done. So we decided to purchase the dress. I handed the dress to the cashier, who asked: "Do you have a coupon?" to which I responded, "No, do you?" Much to our surprise, the cashier opened up a drawer underneath her cash register and scanned a bar code giving us a 20% discount. What a pleasant surprise! I doubt we would have gotten the discount, if I hadn't come back with my question. You get what you ask for; so don't be afraid to ask.

Reflections:
What will give you the courage to ask?
What has held you back from negotiating?

PROVIDING COMMUNITY SERVICES FOR PAY

"A man ought to work. That's what he's here for. That's how
he contributes to the welfare of the community."

~ W. Somerset Maugham, English writer

Would you pay yourself money? This might sound like a strange
question, but stay with me for a bit. My daughter is going to
baby sit a couple of children from a lower grade level next
weekend. She says she has no problem with taking care of the
two children; she also has no problem cooking for them or even
straightening up after them.

But she does have a problem with the *whole money thing*. Her
question to me was: "Why should I get money for not doing anything? I will just be there playing." She was stating her belief that
just watching kids to prevent them from getting into trouble, or
hurting themselves, was A) easy, and B) not worth being paid for.

When you get down to it, my daughter was expressing a notion
of community giving. Community members should help each
other out. And that shouldn't cost anything.

Any mother who reads this will agree with me that watching
kids is not easy. Kids have myriad questions that need answering, they want to explore and be adventurous, they want to
learn, usually the things that adults take for granted. For someone who has raised a family it might be less difficult to watch
children, but it is never easy. It is hard work.

We, as a society, need to start acknowledging the value that
comes with taking care of kids. Just because mothers and fathers

take care of their children for free, their child rearing skills are deemed not valuable. However, there is value in playing with a child, there is value in answering their questions, there is value in cooking with your children and exploring, creating, laughing and listening. When we speak with a child, we never know which conversation is going to be the one that has the most impact on them—the one conversation they will carry into adulthood. Specific incidences I remember will be totally forgotten by my children, but they will remember things, people, occurrences that I would have brushed aside.

What is the value of taking care of a child? I think it's priceless. Each child is unique and has unique qualities. Who is to say that she won't have the key to solving poverty or life on Mars.

Looking back at the dilemma my daughter brought up about being paid for babysitting: Should it be a gift or should the service be paid for? I personally think this is not a matter of *should*. There is no right or wrong, no correct or improper. I think the adult needs to make a decision about what value she is receiving, and the provider of the service and the individual receiving the service need to agree if compensation feels right to both parties.

There are many community services – from watching over children, to shoveling driveways, to neighborhood watch – where the service can be given as a gift or paid for. Neither is more just or more correct than the other.

Reflections:

Think about the services that you provide to your community. Would you pay yourself money for them?

If you were receiving a specific service — one that you are providing for free to those in your family — would you ask for money?

Is there a service that you can provide free of charge to people in your community?

THE TRIALS AND TRIBULATIONS OF BEING AN ENTREPRENEUR

"Innovation is the specific instrument of entrepreneurship...the act that endows resources with a new capacity to create wealth."
~ Peter Drucker, Austrian management writer

Many people dream of being entrepreneurial, independent, focused on their own work and what they are passionate about, but just as self-employment comes with its benefits, so does working as an employee in a corporation.

One of the most common stresses for an entrepreneur is not knowing where the next month's income will come from. It is a feeling new and seasoned entrepreneurs will experience. Having dealt with this for 10 years now, I am increasingly more comfortable with this uncertainty, but it is always in the back of my mind.

Working as an employee for a firm, or company, provides a certain security that cannot be found in entrepreneurship. There is a consistent and dependable paycheck; knowing the fixed amount of money being deposited into your account alleviates the stress of wondering whether next month, or next year, will be profitable.

Creating an entrepreneurship can sometimes make it difficult to plan for the long term. The future may seem bleak if your business venture is in a downturn. And yet, with a small modification to your company's infrastructure, or a change in the market, a business venture that may have seemed bleak can suddenly become prosperous.

Entrepreneurship requires a leap of faith, and an ability to remain positive and resilient. The fact of the matter is that being a business owner is not for everyone, and this isn't a bad or good thing. Some people are more comfortable stepping into the unknown without a safety net; others prefer the comfort of security. Some people need complete control in order to execute their visions, others favor working in a setting where they can collaborate with others and present their work to a supervisor.

It may seem that the grass is greener on the other side. Entrepreneurs envy the security that being an employee provides. Employees envy the freedom and control that owning a business provides. Both positions have their strengths and drawbacks. It is up to you to examine your current situation and decide where you belong.

Reflections:
Which position do you prefer: being an employee or an entrepreneur?
Can you envision yourself on the other side?
Is your current job fulfilling your needs and nurturing your innate talents?
Can working as an employee or becoming an entrepreneur solve the trials and tribulations that you experience in your job?

RELATIONSHIPS

A VISION ABOUT RELATIONSHIPS

"Vision is the art of seeing what is invisible to others."

~ Jonathan Swift

At the beginning of every New Year, newspapers and magazines are full of articles about New Year's resolutions and setting goals. The New Year seems to enable us to start anew with a clean slate and a whole twelve months during which we can make it happen - or so we hope.

In working with my clients, I find people struggling to set goals when the passion and vision is missing. I think it is fair to say that all of us want to live a fulfilled life, whatever this means to each individual. Above and beyond that, we want to make a difference. We want people to know we were on this planet and what impact we had. What does this really mean?

Think of people such as Columbus, Plato, Gandhi, Einstein, Shakespeare, Mozart - the list is huge. All of them had an incredible impact during their lifetime and many have this impact to this day. What do these men have in common? Within their field of interest, and passion, all of them had a vision, an overarching goal that they carried in their soul. This is not to say that they had great personal relationships. But they had a vision.

I attended a teleclass on relationship coaching with Hedy Schleifer, internationally known for her powerful workshops and lectures - see *www.hedyyumi.org*. It was a truly inspiring hour. Hedy presented her *Seven Principles for Conscious Relationships*. Her first and overarching principle centers on relationships living in the space between the I and the THOU. In order for relationships to succeed each partner has to walk across the bridge to the other side, leaving opinions, convictions, egos and suffering behind. Each partner has to come with curiosity and an open mind. The secret is in honoring the *otherness* of the other.

Hedy works with many couples in her workshops. What fascinated me was her vision about taking these principles from individual couples to whole nations. She wants nations around the world to create that safe space in between the I and the THOU with safety and respect.

This vision struck a chord with me, since I am personally passionate about individual communities bridging this gap of understanding, across nations, genders, generations, political and religious divides. Understanding and accepting the differences in THOU – whether it is your partner, your relative, your co-worker or your fellow man – makes it easier to set the stones to build the bridge. Knowing what impact you want to have makes it easy to establish goals.

Reflections:
What about you?
What is your vision?
What is your passion?
What have you always been an advocate for?
What difference do you want to make, this year and in years to come?
What's your legacy?

TRUST YOURSELF

"A man who doesn't trust himself can never truly trust anyone else."

~ Cardinal de Retz, *Memoires*

We seem to need a fresh start as we are going through a very deep worldwide recession. I want to draw attention to a subject near and dear to my heart. I have noticed that communication has been going downhill. Don't get me wrong, it always seems to be a challenge, but as a professional having studied Journalism and having spent much of my adult life focusing on and fine-tuning communication, I do notice a decline. I have often said that most issues in the way of success are communication issues. Communication itself is mostly based on trust. In a high trust environment, communication is open, spontaneous, energizing, fun and real. In a low-trust environment, communication is guarded, closed, and unpleasant, information is withheld and people will misinterpret what's been said. Well, many seemed to have lost trust in our financial institutions, in politicians, in big corporations, the media, in airline security, in people's ability to find jobs, the list goes on. This lack of trust has been earned by above mentioned institutions and people. WE seemed to have lost trust in each other as well. But even more importantly, many seemed to have lost trust in themselves.

Once trust has been lost it can be rebuilt. I remember when my husband and I split up; we had lost all trust in each other and in our relationship. I had also lost trust in myself. I questioned every decision I had ever made and every joint decision we had made. Lack of trust makes for a very hostile environment. You question every statement and don't believe anything anymore. But trust can be rebuilt. How you ask?

Rebuild trust by making commitments and keeping them. If you vowed to keep a food journal, you keep it. If you vowed to work out three times a week, you do. If you vowed to attend three networking events a month, you prioritize that you can attend three events. You start by making commitments to yourself, and you keep them. Until you keep your own commitments, no one will believe you can keep the commitments you have made to others.

It's all about walking the talk. Examine what you are *talking* about. What statements are you making that you want others to believe? Do you believe them yourself? Are you following through with your own commitments? Your trustworthiness depends on two things: Your character and your competence. Are you capable of achieving what you set out to do, and do you have the self-discipline to follow through? Both need to be in place.

In order to improve communication and ultimately trust, we need to walk the talk individually. All of us need to be the best we can be (that doesn't mean perfect!), and follow through with our commitments. No finger pointing allowed though. We need to hold ourselves accountable. Let's start with us and we will have accomplished a lot already.

Reflections:
What will it take for you to trust yourself to do what you are setting out to do?
What requests do you need to make of others around you in order to be able to trust them?

OVER STEPPING

"In every dispute between parent and child, both cannot be right,
but they may be, and usually are, both wrong. It is this situation
which gives family life its peculiar hysterical charm."
~ Isaac Rosenfeld, American writer

My mother grew up with a stepmom she didn't like. My brother
has helped raise three kids as stepdad, in addition to his own
two. My other brother has been a quasi stepdad for a little boy.
I have experienced some of the feelings of having sort of a step-
parent, when my dad entered into another relationship after
my mom passed away. Step relationships are tricky. My brother
reminded me of a German proverb lately, when referring to his
and my relationship: *Blood is thicker than water*, meaning there
is a stronger bond between blood relatives than between other
relationships. I believe this is true. Sometimes that's good and
other times it's not so beneficial. I have observed step relationships for many years now. And I have made a conscious
decision to not subject my kids to that from my end during
their childhood. Now that they are approaching adulthood, I
think they have a strong foundation to deal with anything if and
when it comes up. Have I been overprotective? It may be. In
the end I probably made that choice more for myself then for
them. I just didn't have the bandwidth to deal with children, a
home, and a business while adding a stepdad to the mix. Every
step of the way, I have made decisions that felt right for me and
for us. I know everyone around me is entering into, and getting
out of, relationships based on decisions that feel right. Transitions are messy. Adding or subtracting step relationships can
be messy too. But step relationships can also be very rewarding and beneficial for parent and child. Step relationships are

challenging and need to be handled with care. In the process great relationships can emerge, given a chance. I guess it's all about being open to the learning.

Reflections:
What do you think?
What step relationships have you encountered?
How are they working?
What are you learning from them?

GAINING A NEW PERSPECTIVE

"A definite purpose, like blinders on a horse, inevitably narrows
its possessor's point of view."
~ Robert Frost, American poet

The other day, I was watching my children play chess with each other. Chess being a very strategic game, each player was focused on how to best move toward winning the game, without losing too many pieces along the way. As I was sitting with Susie on one side, I saw her perspective, and recognized the strategy she was implementing. Then I sat with Willy, and recognized that looking at the board from his perspective, the relationship of the pieces on the boards looked totally different. It took me a while to adjust my thinking to the strategy he was implementing, simply because I had a mental imprint from Susie's perspective. After a little while, I saw his patterns emerge. Lastly, I sat watching the board and having Susie and Willy at either side of me, so I wasn't looking at the board from either of their perspectives. What a different perspective altogether. Now, I was more of an objective bystander, able to recognize strategies, and patterns from both of them at the same time. I saw the big picture, and wasn't involved in the detail anymore.

What makes me write about this chess game? It illustrates that when you play chess, you only see one perspective, and the perspective of the side you are on. And it doesn't matter which side you are on, you only see one perspective. But when you step out of the game, and aren't involved in the details, you can see the big picture. One could argue that you are only seeing a third perspective, which is true to an extent. However, not actively being involved in the game gives one more of an objective, unbiased view.

Susie said to me the other day, "Kids' minds are different than parents' minds." She believes parents think differently. I wonder if it's not just like in the chess game. My daughter's perspective is different than mine. Just as anyone else's perspective is different than mine. Your spouse's perspective is different than yours, your boss/employee's perspective is different, as are your friends', and so forth. All of us have very unique perspectives. It's wonderful, because this uniqueness enables us to be creative, and innovative. But we also trip over this uniqueness when it comes to us relating with others. *Why can't he see it my way?* Relationships are strained if the parties in it only see one perspective. Once you have established a certain perspective it is difficult to step out of it. However, I believe in order to grow, learn and advance as a species, we humans need to keep trying to step outside of the game, outside of our comfort zone. We need to be willing to take a risk to try and see the other angle. When you open your mind to the other person's perspective, you allow yourself space to think, analyze and reconsider. How else would we have ever figured out that the earth isn't flat?

Reflections:
What game are you in?
Who are you playing with?
What is your perspective?
What will it take to step out of the game to gain a new perspective?
What positive outcomes can result from your step outside your comfort zone?

AWAKENING YOUR PASSION

"The happiness of a man in this life does not consist in the absence but in the mastery of his passions."
~ Alfred Lord Tennyson, English poet

After I attended the International Coach Federation conference in San Jose, California to learn, connect, and grow, I felt particularly empowered. Why? This conference came on the heels of a yearlong process to build my home while maintaining a full business. And even more importantly, my children are growing and maturing at an incredible rate, which is wonderful and frightening at the same time. Adolescence has a whole new set of challenges!

I showed up at the conference somewhat drained and tired. You would think being surrounded by more than 1,700 coaches, from forty-five countries, would make it worse. Well, it can be intense, but also incredibly fun. It feels like an accelerated coaching workshop where ideas burst forth like fireworks. Being willing to get re-energized, and discovering what's next for me, proved to be very powerful. I met astounding individuals who are willing to explore those ideas with me, not just to create the life we want for our clients, and ourselves, but for humanity.

Following are goals I have set based on this year's conference. I am writing about them, so all of you can remind me going forward:

1. Create Space
2. Serve the Community
3. Raise Awareness

4. Connect People with Resources
5. Break down Cultural Barriers

Attending this conference put me in touch with the possibilities again. I feel like I'm on *Cloud 9* and can't wait to get started. Actually I already have. In our busy world, we yearn to relax and find balance. The balance often proves to be difficult. I discovered the secret is not necessarily to relax, but to rejuvenate, and reenergize. Being surrounded by inspiring, intelligent, thought-provoking, motivated people, and listening to speakers who are visionaries, and activists, did the trick for me. They awakened in me the possibility of positive change on a grand scale. The time you spend with your energizing friends, and relatives, can be utilized, not just for entertainment, but also for your *Cloud 9* experience.

Reflections:
Who do you need or want to connect with?
What will it take to put you on cloud 9 of your life?
What will re-energize you beyond your wildest dreams?
What will awaken your passion beyond belief?

LIFE PARTNER

"A great marriage is not when the 'perfect couple' comes together.
It is when an imperfect couple learns to enjoy their differences."
~ Dave Meurer, Daze of Our Wives

Partnering with another human being is complicated. I have known people who have gotten married and divorced three or four times. Each marriage resulted in a number of kids who are all making the best of it. They share fun moments with their extended families, and sometimes, they fight bitter wars. I also know men and women who have never found a life partner. They look in the mirror at 40, 50, or 60, and wonder. Then there are the happy marriages, where two people made a commitment to go through thick and thin together, and they have. They seem to complement each other, where the sum of all parts is more whole than the individual parts. And then there are the marriages where husband and wife stay together for the kids, or for the house, or the job, or whatever, but they suffer a lifetime of frustration. Who is to say what works best?

I have come to the conclusion there is no right or wrong. There is only what works for the individual in the moment. I was happily married for 12 years, and then I discovered that my husband wasn't who I thought, or believed, he was. I was then unhappily married to him for 4 additional years, crumbling under the weight of the situation. It took another painful 4 years to get divorced.

During the last 6 years, much of my energy has gone to building a new relationship with him, built on trust and mutual respect. Throughout, I have protected, nurtured, and raised two children. Being a single parent brings many challenges, unforeseen traps, and unexpected joys. I feel like I have tried it all: single with career, married in traveling bliss, seeing the dark side of others (but mostly my own), and coming out on the other end, intact. The journey has made me stronger, and more resilient. If I had the opportunity to do it all over again, I wouldn't change a thing. I feel well equipped to explore the world, and enjoy my journey, as I am embarking on the second half of my life. I wonder what new adventures wait for me with, or without, a partner. Who knows?

SETTING BOUNDARIES

"Givers have to set limits, because takers rarely do."

~ Irma Kurtz, *Cosmopolitan Magazine*

Have you ever felt irritated when the people around you do not respect your time? They don't treat you the way you want to be treated? Maybe they even yell at you? Have you ever felt taken advantage of by your children, or used by your boss? I am sure you can identify with at least one of these scenarios.

Are you hurt, angry, irritated, or resentful around certain people, because of the way they have treated you? You feel really upset with them, and it feels natural to want to blame them, and make it their fault. But, if you are honest with yourself, the real truth is that you are upset with YOU for allowing them to treat you this way? It's all about not setting appropriate and strong boundaries.

Boundaries are rules that we communicate to others about what we will, or will not, accept from them. Boundaries are what you have decided that other people or environments cannot do to you. In other words, boundaries are basically a NO!

No, you cannot dump that task on me.
No, you cannot be rude to me.
No, you cannot schedule a meeting during this time with me.
No, you may not yell at me.

See, if you can see your own behavior in one of these categories:

The Overpromiser
Is your life chaotic and crazy? Are you always late? Do you have

trouble managing your time? You are probably an Overpromiser. You find yourself taking on way more than you need to. The Overpromiser finds it is almost impossible to say NO when someone asks them to take on another volunteer leadership role, or another project at their child's school. In the workplace, the Overpromiser says yes to everything out of fear for losing the job or the next promotion. Also, the Overpromiser doesn't think they are allowed to change their mind once they have agreed to do something.

The Perpetual Pleaser
If you are afraid of making anyone upset with you, then you probably are a Perpetual Pleaser. Because Perpetual Pleasers are very sensitive, they don't like having other people getting upset with them (for any reason), so they set up their lives so no one becomes unhappy.

The Perfectionist
The Perfectionist lives to create the image of perfection. This is the image they want others to have of them, and the image they want to have of themselves. Perfect people can handle everything, and consequently, they have trouble admitting to anyone they need help, or are overburdened.

So, how do we go about setting boundaries with the people around us?

1. *Clearly identify your boundaries for yourself* and know when they are being challenged, or overstepped. Ask yourself, what specific behavior is causing me discomfort? Is it reasonable to expect the behavior to stop? Is it an issue from the past? If so, deal with it. Start setting the boundary.

2. *Inform the offending person about the behavior you find unacceptable and ask them to stop.* Don't expect them to know, because they don't. You have to tell them, because they can't read your mind. Don't bring the subject up in the middle of an argument. Pick a time, when the subject can be discussed very matter-of-factly. Just ask them to stop. For example, if you want meetings to start on time, say that you expect the meeting to start promptly.

3. *State the consequence of their behavior if they do not stop.* For example, you will not wait for latecomers to start the meeting. They might miss out on important information. Without stating the consequence, you are simply nagging, which will waste your time by having to do it over and over again. And you will not get what you want. Make sure you are willing to deliver the consequence, and make it situation appropriate.

4. *Remind them once if the behavior occurs again.* They might not be used to you making requests in an assertive manner. Because you are in control, there is no need to get angry.

5. *If the behavior continues, follow through with the consequence.* Beware of empty threats. Empty threats are consequences you are not willing to enforce. Your children are excellent at testing you on this one. If you don't follow through on the consequence, you have lost the battle.

Reflections:
Take inventory of your relationships with your family, friends, at school and at work.
Do you need to set some boundaries?

YOU AS A MEMBER OF YOUR COMMUNITY

"The community stagnates without the impulse of the individual."

~ William James, *Great Men, Great Thoughts, and the Environment*

Have you asked yourself lately what communities you are in? In my recent travels, I had conversations with people from the US, France, Germany, England, Mexico, Canada, Rwanda, India and China.

I have taken inventory of the communities I am a part of. The conversations in each community are rich and inspiring. There is the global executive community, the Thunderbird community, the Mount Madonna School community, the coaching community, and my local community to name a few. I have started asking myself as to the role that I am fulfilling in each community. Am I participating, leading, or merely present to be informed? I have decided to intentionally pick three communities to focus on. The intention is to become a viable contributor to each community, regardless of what role I am taking on. Being an attentive listener is important and so is taking on leadership functions. The best leaders are excellent listeners as well. The key is to be aware of what your function is.

Reflections:

What communities am I a part of?

What is my contribution?

Where can I make the most out of my gifts and talents?

Where can I have the greatest impact given my resources and constraints?

Where can I emerge as a leader?

It's perfectly ok to be a follower in some communities, but challenge yourself to be a leader in some others.

Can you imagine the problems we could solve as humankind, if everyone had the mindset of leadership, and became engaged in the leadership of the communities where they can make the most difference? Isn't it at least desirable in order to be a good citizen?

WHAT CONVERSATION DO YOU WANT TO INITIATE?

*"A single conversation across the table with a wise person
is worth a month's study of books."*
~ Chinese Proverb

I attended a conference, called CAM, in beautiful Asheville, North Carolina. I have been to many conferences, where the usual format includes keynote speeches from well-known and respected experts in their fields, followed by breakout sessions one can choose from. Typically, you are confined to your chair and spoken to, and if you are lucky you have an engaging speaker who captures your imagination. Sometimes you just have to endure, or you leave and pick a different break out session. CAM, Conversation Among Masters, was refreshingly different. The Grove Park Inn, a stunning resort overlooking the Blue Ridge Mountains, provided a relaxing and beautiful environment. I loved the idea of rocking chairs everywhere. As a matter of fact, for one of the sessions we were all sitting in rocking chairs. How fun!

What really struck me though, was that aside from the program keeping us busy all day, we were fully engaged throughout the day. Rather than being talked to, we were having conversations all day long, over breakfast with colleagues, during the morning with a guest who introduced a specific topic. The guest served as a foundation to engage in conversation with him or her. Over lunch we would deepen the discussions with our peers and bring back ideas for the larger group to discuss. This format allowed us to deepen a subject or topic, and broaden our awareness by listening to, or expressing, different points of view. Not only did we make deeper connections, but we gained insights we wouldn't have had, had we simply been talked to. Previously, I would leave a conference full in my mind, but somehow depleted. This time, I left feeling energized and inspired, with lots of ideas and dreams. I made great friends and can't wait to continue the conversations with them.

This experience made me think about how we communicate in everyday life. In the morning everyone rushes out the door, we call others, and leave voicemail messages. We send email and text messages. On our way to work, only a few people carpool, and most cars only carry the driver. When we take the train, everyone is occupied with their own thoughts. When we arrive at the office, people spend more time on the computer than talking with others. Anyone lucky enough to be able to work from home is craving human interaction or become stir crazy.

Whatever happened to the art of conversation? It's valuable for our wellbeing, but we are losing this skill. If you look at the next generation the trend becomes even more obvious. Today's teenagers are capable of multitasking with lots of electronic devices, but do they know how to converse? I believe our brains need it, our hearts yearn for it, and our souls crave it.

There is a German tradition called *Stammtisch*. In many German restaurants, especially the long established ones, you will find a large table in the corner with a plaque identifying the *Stammtisch*. This table is an open invitation to locals, but usually others are welcome to sit together and talk, sometimes daily, or sometimes once a week. The *Stammtisch* is my reminder to continue the art of conversation. Why else would there be so many book clubs, knitting groups, tailgate parties, and networking events?

But conversation takes time, and time is precious. Don't let the art of conversation die. Ask yourself how you can incorporate more conversation into your life. Take a break and stroll down to the water cooler, stop eating lunch at your desk, start a discussion group or a book club, take the time to talk to your neighbor, have coffee with a friend, have dinner with your family, turn off the computer or TV, and go for a walk with a friend.

Reflections:
Who do I want to have a conversation with today?
What conversation do I want to initiate?

DO AWAY WITH JUDGEMENT

"When you judge another, you do not define them, you define yourself."

~ Wayne Dyer, *American author & lecturer*

I have been wondering lately why we seem so fascinated with TV shows that judge people, such as *Survivor, American Idol* or *Dancing with the Stars*. What is the attraction? In each one of these shows, people get judged, but why is this so fascinating? What is it about judgement? I looked up the word *judgement* and one definition I found on the web was *the cognitive process of reaching a decision or drawing conclusions*. Let's face it - we make judgements all the time. We decide who we like, who we want to be around, whom we want to allow into our circle. Similarly, we decide whom we don't like, or whom we don't want to be associated with. But how can we be certain we draw the right conclusions? How can we be certain we aren't pigeonholing or judging people based on our assumptions?

Let's assume for a moment, everyone we come in contact with, even more so, every person in this world, is doing the best they can in each moment, given their circumstances. We can't really ask for more, can we? If everyone does their best, what's there to judge, and who are we to judge? What gives us the right to say person A is better than person B? This is very subjective, and really doesn't take into consideration the place each individual came from, or what hurdles they have had to overcome.

Wouldn't it make more sense to celebrate everybody's accomplishments for what they are worth, and by doing so build up people's confidence and self-esteem? Just think of the possibilities if every person was confident instead of deflated by criticism and judgement. We are naturally very hard on ourselves; wouldn't it be nice to hear a friendly voice acknowledging things we did well, instead of highlighting what didn't work so well? That is not to say that we don't need to own up to our own mistakes and learn from them.

Reflections:
What can each and every one of us do to reduce judgement? What can you do to accept people for who they are rather than judge them?

Take a moment to think of someone in the forefront of your mind who you have been judging. What is your judgement based on - fact or fiction? Which questions do you need to ask to get more clarity? Will you be able to ask him/her? Can you come up with two more right now? Think of the impact you could have by acknowledging someone's efforts rather than judging them. Think of the possibilities.

If you want to hone this skill even more, read a newspaper or a book that takes an opposite political standpoint to your own. Rather than reading it in order to prove how right you are and how wrong they are, try to understand what might make them take such a viewpoint. The aim is to understand, not to persuade or be persuaded.

Are you able to hold your opinions and views as legitimate at the same time you hold others' views as equally legitimate? Are you still able to even if you don't agree?

WITNESSING

"To understand the heart and mind of a person, look not at what
he has already achieved, but at what he aspires to do."
~ Khalil Gibran, Lebanese philosopher

Recently, I re-discovered that I have a very observing mind.
I am not at my best being the performer, even though I can
be the performer if need be. I am at my best, however, when
I get to witness and when I get to be present with my clients,
my peers, my family, and friends. I am at my best when I am
allowed to witness, much like an eagle from the sky, the beauty
of human beings, nature, and life.

I am fortunate to be able to hold the vessel for the personal and
professional growth of my clients. I appreciate when my advice
is sought but not required, when my sheer presence makes a difference, when my energy grounds people and heals and soothes
their wounds. I am lucky to be a trusted partner. Thank you to all
who are allowing me to witness their amazing presence.

Reflections:
Are you a witness?
Who do you get to observe?
Are you trying to solve problems and fix thing or people, or are
you there, witnessing their advances and listening to their
concerns?
What part do you want to play in the development of the peo-
ple around you?
What part do you want them to play in your development?
Let me encourage you to not only reflect on this topic, but
to actually engage in conversations around this with your
friends and family. You might just be surprised.

CREATING MEMORIES TO LAST BOTH YOUR LIFETIMES

"What greater thing is there for two human souls than to feel that
they are joined ... to strengthen each other ... to be one
with each other in silent unspeakable memories."
~ George Eliot, *Adam Bede*

To all parents - no matter how old your children are. And to all children no matter how old your parents are - this is for you.

When I first came home with the idea to walk a half-marathon with my friends, my daughter Susie, 11-years-old, said: "Can I go?" I was caught a bit by surprise since I never considered she was up for something like that. We signed up and trained as much as we could between school, homework, and other scheduled activities. We discovered the time on our walks was well spent with some great conversations between mother and daughter. As we approached the day of the event, I wasn't sure how far we were going to make it. Equipped with a cell phone for emergency pick up and plenty of food and water, we set out to join 9,000 other participants. The first seven miles seemed to go by fairly easily despite the hilly nature of San Francisco. Not having a mile marked between mile 7 and 9 almost broke Susie's spirit, but by the time we passed mile marker 9, we were over 2/3rds of the way toward our goal, so she kept going. I guess she was looking forward to the Giradelli chocolate to be handed out at mile 12. Little did we know that all the chocolate would be gone by the time we got there. It was hard for Susie and I to walk over all the empty wrappers! She marched across the finish line after 13.1 miles with her spirits high and she was incredibly happy. We were both proud of our accomplishment, and more importantly, we got to succeed together. We got to spend a little over 3 1/2 hours together cheering each other on, discussing our emotions along the way. What a great time spent together! Nothing else mattered, we were totally in the moment. No thought of homework or bills to pay, deadlines, or responsibilities. We were focused on the goal and pooled our resources to get there. I am extremely grateful to have had the opportunity to share this experience with my daughter. A memory of a lifetime neither one of us will forget.

We do so many things for and with our children that we hope they will remember later—a special birthday party, a great vacation, an event. We wonder which events they will remember.

Reflections:
Which events/experiences can you create with your children and parents that will last a lifetime, which ones will create lasting memories of great time spent together - truly in the moment?
Ask your children and/or parents what experiences they remember.

BRIDGING CULTURAL DIVIDES

"I do not want my house to be walled in on all sides and my windows to be stuffed. I want the cultures of all the lands to be blown about my house as freely as possible."
~ Mahatma Ghandi, *Indian philosopher*

Typically, people talk about culture in the context of different countries or nationalities. There are different cultural contexts among the European countries, Asia, the Middle East, and so forth. Language, dress, and food customs vary. We have all heard of different greetings, different space requirements, and different perceptions in regards to just about anything.

So, when I say there is a cultural war in the United States, what am I talking about? The concept of a cultural war was really made clear to me when I watched a TV program about code words. The argument was made that if a person is told after an interview *he is not a fit here*, a black person will receive this message differently than a white person. To a black person, it is an immediate reference to his color, which is not at all the message a white person will receive. A white person will, most likely, think he just doesn't have the right qualifications for the job.

What I realize more and more lately is that we are surrounded by cultural conflicts. Let me give you some examples about cultural divides I have recently seen:

- A German company doing business in China
- Two companies with different belief structures and values merging

- Non-profits not understanding how business is conducted in the for profit world and vice versa
- Parents not understanding their teenagers and vice versa
- The entrepreneur community feeling not needed by the academic community
- Lack of understanding between two different religions
- A former corporate executive entering the world of entrepreneurs
- An east coast company trying to acquire a west coast company with different beliefs

What is culture? The difficulty with describing culture is that it is always changing. To me, culture describes who I am and what matters most to me. It shapes my attitudes, my behaviors and how I act in different environments. My culture is shaped by my upbringing, but it gets shifted by what communities I am a part of, the company I work for, or the business I run, the school I send my children to, the gender or race I am, the place I live in, and who I associate with. Our individual culture is shaped daily by what is meaningful, or important, who we are in the world, and in relation to others.

I believe our culture is, to a large extent, shaped by our language. Certain German words have a certain meaning in the German cultural context, and the same holds true in any other language. Not always do they translate well, especially since each word has associations that are particular to the culture. Certain words and phrases have certain meaning depending on what cultural beliefs we are part of (i.e. black, white, male, female, gay, straight, corporate, entrepreneur, old, young, and so forth.)

Coming back to the culture war in the US: Regardless of what side of the political aisle you sit on, you will respond positive to language that is aligned with your own cultural beliefs. Language, and the way it's used, seems more important than the issues being talked about in any election.

I had never heard the phrase *Joe Six-Pack* before the Obama/McCain election, a new phrase to attach an association to. Someone said he associates the term with: male, white, and hunter with a dog. This explanation defined the term *Joe Six-pack* for me. Is it correct? I have no idea. I was unable to find a Merriam Webster dictionary definition. I hope it demonstrates my point though. I will make this association from now on until someone gives me a different explanation. That's what happens to all of us. As we grow up and learn our language we associate certain images to our words. It furthers our understanding and at the same time it taints our belief and limits us to reverse or change our understanding. But these beliefs lead to conflict and misunderstanding, especially in a population of 300 million. The McCain/Obama presidential race beautifully demonstrated different cultural beliefs among blacks, whites, men, women, old, young, educated, and blue collar - the list goes on.

I am passionate about bridging cultural divides because I believe our intolerance of different cultures keep us from living peacefully and united on this planet of ours. The possibility of overcoming the existing beliefs of one culture and collaboration with another culture, are endless and provide mental, spiritual, and material wealth. Coaching is a process to question what we believe is true. At times, it makes us feel uncomfortable, but it always offers new awareness and realizations. We tend to be prisoners of our own thoughts. Just think of the possibility of being able to escape that mental custody and feel that freedom that invariably shows up. Scary, yes, but absolutely worth it!

Reflections:
How can we bridge different cultures?
How do we reduce conflict in our daily interactions, communities, and the world?
What questions do you want to ask about cultural divides?
What conversations do you want to have about cultural divides?

WHAT DIFFERENT PERSPECTIVE CAN YOU EXPLORE?

"The real voyage of discovery consists not in seeking
new lands but in seeing with new eyes."

~ Marcel Proust, *French thinker*

Throughout my years coaching, I have recognized that during certain times there are similar themes that emerge amongst my clients. I try to sit back and see what themes and patterns surface. One week, I had two clients that actually used the exact same phrase to describe an experience, but in completely different contexts. Both of them were describing a *whole other world* that they got to experience while traveling. Interestingly, one had traveled from Los Angeles (urban) to Tennessee (rural), whereas the other had traveled from the San Francisco Bay Area (suburb) to Chicago (city). And yet, both were describing a similar experience in the sense of it being eye opening and energizing. They described the different landscape, the people, the clothes, the tools and the cars. Both recognized that this new environment gave them a new point of view of what is.

One definition of *perspective* in the dictionary is *a mental view, outlook, or prospect.* Our perspective, our mental view, is what we think of as reality. We recognize different perspectives when we travel, and yet we don't have to travel so far. Our neighbor has a different perspective from ours; and even our family members have a different view of reality. It is easy for us to assume that everyone around us observes the same reality, when, in fact, none of us do! Sometimes we notice this after we send an e-mail and receive a totally different response than anticipated. No wonder! The recipient's reality is different from ours.

I want to encourage you to explore different perspectives. Go to a different part of town, one you usually don't go to, or travel some other place, and observe what you see. Ask friends, and family members about their points of view on a particular issue, and just listen. Try to understand the mental view of your spouse, your boss, your child, or a friend, and observe what you are finding. It can be an eye opening experience. The reason why we don't all agree on political or religious issues, for example, is because we have been exposed to different views. The key is to be aware that all of us have different perspectives. Through communication and conversation we can open the door to understanding. First we need to accept that we all have different angles on things, and then, we need to start to understand each other's perspectives by open communication.

Reflections:
Start a conversation with a friend. Know your stance, but don't state it. Just sit back, listen, and recognize how different the perspectives can be.

LOOK PAST THE FRUSTRATION

"Anger makes you smaller, while forgiveness forces you
to grow beyond what you were."
~ Cherie Carter-Scott, If Love is a Game, These are the Rules

Let's see if you can relate to the following scenario: You have made a specific request of a coworker, a family member, and a friend. Nothing happens. You follow up by repeating your request and still nothing happens. You get frustrated. It seems so simple. Why can't she give you the information you need to move forward? You get tired of asking. Now, you are getting angry with her. What's up with her?

This month one such scenario unfolded in my life. I was extremely frustrated and didn't know what else to do to get the information, which I had been seeking for months. I felt stuck and this seemingly simple issue was draining my energy - big time!

To the best of my knowledge one person was holding the key to the resolution of the problem. I was a victim! However, I was through being a victim. I didn't want to be a victim anymore, so I started asking others for their thoughts on the subject. Well, no one else could think of an alternative solution. In a conversation with my coach, I recognized that I had focused all of my energy toward this one person.

What if I were to broaden my view more? Who else might be able to get me toward the needed information? This sounds so simple writing it down now – but at the time it was a real stretch. I couldn't think of anyone else I knew who might have the information I needed. All of a sudden, I thought of this very remote possibility; someone I knew 25 years ago, who I had completely lost touch with, might know.

Well, it took some time and effort, but I did connect with her and - can you believe it - she was able to give me the information I was seeking. Who would have thought? Well, I didn't initially. Truly thinking outside the box made it possible.

What about the person who didn't respond to my request initially? I was angry with him because he could have saved me time, trouble, and in fact, money. But then could he have really? From my perspective, - yes, but from his perspective, obviously not. Otherwise, he would have given me the information. Something was holding him back. After much thought, I have come to the conclusion that given each moment in time, he has done the best he could, even when it didn't seem that way to me. Who am I to judge? What do I know about the pressure placed upon him by himself or others? Have I ever walked in his shoes? From my perspective, giving me the information seemed easy, but from his perspective?

Bottom-line: I got the information I needed and I was able to move on.

Reflecting on this episode for some time now, I was able to forgive him; he did the best he could. Don't all of us all the time? Coming from a place of kindness and compassion helped me forgive him. I for my part feel complete.

Reflections:

Is there anyone in your life you need to forgive regardless of how right you think you are?

What seemingly unsolvable problem can you tackle?

Who else can you utilize as a resource?

What do you need to enable you to think outside of the box?

YOU CAN EXPERIENCE GRATITUDE EVERY DAY

"Gratitude is not only the greatest of virtues, but the parent of all others."
~ Cicero, Roman philosopher

These times of uncertainty make us fearful, but, if you allow it, also humble and appreciative! My clients, and many of my friends, have brought up the notion of gratitude in one form or another. One client was grateful for having a job, enabling him to provide for his family at a time when few jobs in this economy are secure. Another was grateful about having a healthy family, and being healthy himself. Yet another client shifted from saying "I have to do this." to "I get to do this," which made a huge difference for her. Again, another client was grateful for having a close relationship with his children. Being able to connect to a sense of gratitude for those around you, and the good fortune you have, is irreplaceable and beneficial.

When we are grateful, we appreciate the love and beauty around us during that moment. We aren't concerned with what happened in the past and who is to be blamed for it. At the same time, we are not concerned with what might take place in the future. The feeling of gratefulness transports us to where life is worth living - in the moment.

I had an interesting experience. My mother-in-law was taken to the hospital, after she had a heart attack. After some complications, she was moved into the Intensive Care Unit. Because the situation was quite serious, her children and their spouses gathered in the hospital. Emotions were strained, and the topic of discussion centered on what had happened in the past (when she had had the heart attack) or how she was doing since she arrived in the hospital. The big *what if* questions were also debated: *What if* this treatment doesn't work? *What if* her blood pressure goes up or down? *What if* she dies?

Then it was my turn to see her. I have been to ICU's before and felt prepared. However, the sight of a loved one hooked up to machines and tubes, is shocking every time. Once I was past the initial unease, I remembered to tap into my feelings of gratitude, and put aside the negativity. I was grateful for having met her twenty-two years ago, and having her as my *American* mother for that length of time. I was grateful for her love and generosity, her caring, and gracious giving, and just for being who she is. It put me right into the moment. I wasn't worried about the past or any issues we might have had to deal with. I wasn't worried about the future, because her body was going to do what it needed to do. I was present with her and it was peaceful. No matter which way her body was going to go, it was going to be just right. I never gave up hope, and yet, I wasn't dependent on it either. The experience felt light and almost joyful.

What if we lived every moment of every day, completely in the present? I would call this LIVING!

Reflections:
What are you grateful for?
Who in your life brings you joy and happiness?
Which memories, traits, or good fortunes enable you to tap
into your gratitude and leave your negativity aside?
How can you replicate this feeling over and over again? Con-
sider starting a gratitude journal. Everyday write down a

list of people and aspects of your life that you are grateful for. Try to add a new point every day. You may realize that the more you think about gratitude, the more you realize you have what to be grateful for and the easier it is to access your gratitude and replicate the emotion every day.

DON'T GIVE A GIFT, RETURN ONE

"The best and most beautiful things in the world cannot be seen
or even touched. They must be felt within the heart."

~ Helen Keller, *The Story of my Life*

I had the opportunity to attend the annual International Coaching Federation Conference in Atlanta. Among many fabulous speakers, I was also fortunate to be able to attend Ken Blanchard's closing keynote address about what he has learned from coaching. Ken Blanchard is the author of books including, *The One Minute Manager, Gung Ho and Raving Fans,* and is a consultant and speaker to companies such as *Microsoft, Honda, Eastman Kodak,* and *General Motors.*

Among many excellent points, the one thing he said that stuck with me fits with the year-end. When we approach Thanksgiving and Christmas, we are often asked to reflect and give thanks in the form of thank yous, and also, in form of money. Many times we go through the motions and don't really think about it. Ken pointed out that he hates the word *GIVING*. It is so close to the concept of *giving up* that you feel as if you are giving up something of your own by giving. He much prefers the term *RETURNING*. Think about this for a moment. If we are returning rather than giving, we aren't actually giving anything up at all. We are actually giving back something we already received. What a great distinction!

This ties together beautifully with an exercise we did in one of the break out sessions at the conference. We were asked to confer with a colleague to identify the qualities of leaders that we had had the privilege to work for, and with, in the past. First of all, I discovered that it is truly a privilege to work for/and with leaders. Not everybody feels this way about his or her boss, mentor, father, mother, and so forth. Second of all, I discovered that in many cases, I had taken their leadership for granted. They had touched my life and in many ways, I had never gone back to acknowledge them for the inspiration and guidance I had received from them.

Reflections:
Who has been touching your life, who has been guiding you and who has blessed you with a vision in your life? Pick three to five of them and acknowledge them for the impact they have had on your life.

You might have to research, to discover where they live now, write a letter, pick up the phone, or just tell them in person. What a gift to RETURN! You might be surprised by some of the reactions you get.

HAVE YOU TAKEN A RISK TO PUT YOURSELF AHEAD?

"Right now I feel like I can do pretty much anything!"

~ Susie Bryan, My daughter

The school my daughter Susie is attending in the Santa Cruz Mountains has a strong performing arts program. The first week of school, the entire middle school went on a 4-day trip to the Marine Headlands Institute, north of San Francisco, to research marine wild life and to have a bonding and team building experience.

During the second week of school the teachers set aside time for song sharing. Each student had to come prepared to sing a song *a capella* in front of all the middle school students. A terrifying thought to me personally! Apparently the apple doesn't fall to far from the tree, since this was pretty terrifying for Susie, as well. During the summer she had picked a song, and practiced it over, and over, but she was very stressed because she didn't know what to expect. She had presented reports in front of class, but singing a song seemed to take fear to a new level. Each day, Susie would come home saying that the 8th graders got to go first, or they ran out of time. Finally, she got to share her song, as the last person!

She told me how petrified she was getting up in front of everybody. Once she was done, she was carried by this feeling of elation of actually having done it. It didn't matter if it was perfect or not - she had done it! Cloud 9 was nothing in comparison! She was proud, and many of her classmates cheered her on, giving her high 5's. Once she was home, I asked her how she felt, and she said: "Mom, right now I feel like I can do pretty much anything!" She described how terrifying it had been to face being embarrassed, but she felt great about stepping out of her comfort zone. She loved the feeling of accomplishment. I know she will, in the future, continue to step outside of her comfort zone again, and again.

Kids are asked to take risks all the time - it is part of the learning process. What about adults? When was the last time you let yourself be vulnerable, and you came out ahead? If you haven't done it lately, I'd like to encourage you to seek out opportunities where you; too, can step outside of your comfort zone. It could be telling someone how you truly feel. It may be taking a relationship to another stage - whether it is marriage or divorce. It could be pushing emotions of resentment aside and opening up the channels for forgiveness with an estranged friend, or family member. Taking chances, and being daring, means being proactive with your life, rather than reactive. if you want to take control of your life - then go for it, take a chance and enjoy the ride!

FROM HEAD TO HEART

"Gratitude is the memory of the heart."

~ Italian Proverb

I had been going through a busy time. I went to the International Coaching Conference in Quebec, and there I attended two book club meetings, watched the movie *What the bleep do we know?*, coached my clients, took an exam, attended an opening ceremony at my kids' school, sewed my daughter's costume for 'Oklahoma', attended a family event at the local Museum of Art and History, went to the dentist, had meetings with contractors practically every day, and the list goes on. Is your head spinning yet? Mine was! It made me stop and think, 'was I trying to do it all'? Most certainly. I didn't want to miss a beat and to live life to the fullest. But was this what it was all about? Can you relate to what I am describing?

I am grateful, because I have myriad opportunities, opportunities that, frankly, the majority of people in this world don't have. And yet, there I was, exhausted from doing it all. I decided it was time to regroup and refocus. What was most important to me? How could I get from my head to my heart?

Here is what works for me:

1. Gratitude:
Gratitude makes me humble. Gratitude makes me reach out to people. It makes me feel good, and it has a ripple effect toward others. How do we show our gratitude? Generally, by saying thank you: Thank you for your support, thank you for helping me take care of this and thank you for being there for

me. What unique ways of saying thank you can you come up with? Have you ever written a letter to your local newspaper thanking your neighbor? Have you ever publicly thanked someone for a job well done, or just for being who they are? Every time you say the words Thank You, do you mean them from the bottom of your heart?

2. Contribution:

What about contribution? I want to live my life making a contribution every day - to my family, my clients, my friends, to my business partners, and so forth. I want to be able to put a smile on people's faces. That makes me smile. Try asking yourself every morning: How am I going to contribute today? How am I going to make a difference? Can I make someone feel special by acknowledging them on their birthday? Can I make a decision today that will impact hundreds of people positively? The sky is the limit.

What I want for all of you is the ability to be grateful and to make a contribution. It's not about doing, doing, doing, it's all about being who you are - and you are best at that!

May your true light shine through - and beyond!

COMMUNITY IS THE KEY
"For a community to be whole and healthy,
it must be based on people's love and concern for each other."
~ Millard Fuller, *Founder of Habitat for Humanity*

In honor of my newly finished home, I held a *Barn Raising/Richtfest*. In order to prepare for this celebration, I thought about what this ceremony is all about.

Traditionally, a barn raising in America is an event where the local community gets together in order to raise the walls of a neighbor's barn, collaboratively. Of course, physically raising the walls, and creating the space, is a huge accomplishment. The completion of the task is celebrated with great fanfare. Thinking about this tradition, I realized the key is the community. No one person is doing it alone. Everyone is coming together to work, and providing their own resources to get the task done.

In Germany, a slightly different tradition has a similar effect. After the roof timbers of a new home have been set, a little pine tree is mounted on top of the roof to symbolize the reaching of the top. The community, consisting of the homeowner and the contractors, as well as friends and family, get together to celebrate and honor the people who contributed to the creation of the new space.

The community works together as a team to reach the goal and get the task done. In the process, the team collaborates, and only by everyone pitching in, does the job get completed. The ceremony gives everyone a chance to reflect on their accomplishments, and a chance to acknowledge and give back to the community.

What community are you a part of? Your company? Your department? Your friends? Your family? Are you working side by side, or are you working as a team? We often think of a team as part of a work environment, or in a sports setting. But what about the team of people you surround yourself with as an individual - your physician, your hairdresser, your personal trainer, your babysitter? They are all part of your team, your community. You work together on common goals, your good health, looking and feeling good, a product launch, a new installation, a tennis tournament, the successful parenting of your children, and so on.

Have you heard of the saying: *It takes a village to raise a child*? It doesn't stop when we reach adulthood. We still need our community to thrive.

So, we all have a community. When do we stop and take the time to celebrate, not only the completion of the job, but celebrate the effort put forth by the individual members of the community? The only way to acknowledge, and honor, them is by being in the moment. You cannot deeply appreciate someone, if you are already running off to the next task, and stressed because of it. What other ways are there to honor people and their efforts? How about a hug and a heartfelt thank you? How about a public thank you to give recognition in front of the team?

Reflections:

Who is in your community and how can you honor those who contribute to the common goal on a daily basis.

How can you celebrate?

What ritual or ceremony can you put in place that would honor the people in your community?

FINDING ROLE MODELS IN THE MOST UNEXPECTED PLACES

"Each person must live their life as a model for others."

~ Rosa Parks, *civil rights activist*

One of my executive clients, who is not married and doesn't have any children, said something to me that made me stop for a second. He said that being a leader and managing people, would be easier if he had children. He thought that the kind of communication necessary in day-to-day life of a family would have prepared him for some of the problems he is encountering in dealing with his employees.

We can learn a lot from our children. Children by nature live in the moment, are curious, want to be and do their best, and they want to learn. Above all, they want to play and have fun. Aren't those the qualities we would like our employees to have as well? Somehow, from the time we are little, to being a fully functioning grown-up, we tend to forget all these positive things. We tend to stress from one appointment to the next. I wouldn't call that living in the moment, would you? We don't seem to give ourselves time to be curious and explore new ideas, because we are stressed about an upcoming deadline. We want to be and do our best. But our expectations of ourselves are so high that we beat ourselves up for not being good enough. When do we take the time to learn something new, either by attending a training class, learning about another department, or discovering how other companies deal with the same issues? When we learn to hold the sense of wonder and curiosity that is so present in children, we learn to laugh and play at work. In this economy, where employees are so concerned about keeping their jobs, we should look to the unexpected role model to find inspiration and encouragement. Children can be that source.

At this point I want to give credit to my two children. They have each written a poem, which I want to share with you, because we can all learn from them:

A Poem on the Glistening Lake

I was in front of the most beautiful lake, my worst enemy, and yet, I didn't want to jump in. I usually feared all the fish in this lake, drowning, the water plants tangling up in my feet. But this time, I feared touching the bottom and hurting something, a fish, some water plants. I took a look into the water and saw darkness, total darkness. I seemed to swirl into imagination, a different world, but then I snapped back. I closed my eyes and stepped at the side of my feared enemy. One, Two, Three! I jumped forward and seemed to be stranded there in the air for several minutes, as I looked into the lake.

Then I plummeted into the cool water and came up to the surface, not as scared as I used to be. I hadn't touched the bottom and I hadn't hurt anything.

I felt so good that I had accomplished this!
~ By Susie Bryan

So, when are you going to jump into the cold water and face your worst enemy?

Willy

There once was a boy named Willy who always was very silly then one day a dog came to play oh that lucky boy named Willy
~ *By Willy Bryan*

When was the last time you were silly? When did you last play with a dog or other pet?

Reflections:
Who is your role model?
Which people around you possess traits that you would like
to have?

EMOTIONAL WELL-BEING

CAN YOU BE THE KEY TO YOUR SUCCESS?

"A man is a success if he gets up in the morning and goes to bed
at night and in between does what he wants to do."
~ Bob Dylan, American poet and musician

I would like to share a story with you that had a profound impact on me and culminated in an inspirational experience for me and some of my friends.

A few years back, a mother of two in our local Montessori community, set out to reach a big goal. She wanted to hike up Halfdome at Yosemite National Park with a group of female friends. Hiking Halfdome is quite a challenge, and takes much preparation, physically and mentally. For Carolee, however, it was an even bigger goal, since having battled with cancer, making it to the top would be a special celebration of life. She was in remission at the time, and thought she could reach her goal. However, she became quite ill right before the trip was to take place, and the whole group decided to cancel the adventure. Carolee passed away that summer. She was survived by her husband and two wonderful children. We happily remember her love for life!

The following year, we decided to climb Halfdome in Carolee's honor. It was the least we could do to preserve her wishes. Despite being mothers of young children, sacrificing Mother's Day weekend was not even an issue. From January on, we planned, trained, organized, wondered, and prepared ourselves to reach our goal. There were many obstacles. For family reasons, some women had to drop out; others were willing to step in. Then, we discovered we couldn't actually climb

Halfdome. Due to the late snowfall that year, the trail was actually closed. Even that didn't deter us from reaching our goal. We decided to hike up Northdome in Yosemite National Park instead. It is an equally challenging 18-mile hike with 3,500 feet ascent offering some outstanding panoramic views. As we reached the summit, after losing the trail in the snow and a longer than normal ascent, we paused and remembered Carolee who was with us, in spirit. Eight of us traveled to Yosemite in her honor. She was with us that day, as we laughed and cried, soaked in the incredible beauty, and watched the wildlife. We hiked for a staggering 12 hours and reached the valley floor after sunset—exhausted, tired, with blistered feet, and sun burned faces. None of us will ever forget that day!

What was the key to our success? Was the key to success good equipment, such as good boots, light backpacks, appropriate clothing, and detailed maps? Was the key to success good time management to assure that we would get off the mountain, before it got dark? Was the key to success good communication to make sure that everyone knew exactly what we were in for? Was the key to success good leadership and trust?

While all these things were certainly important factors in a successful hike, there may be one factor that's easily overlooked. Even with perfect equipment, good time management, great communication and leadership, we might not have succeeded. The REAL key to success lay within each one of us hikers.

US. It all began and ended with us. It wasn't the people, or circumstances around us. Each one of us was motivated, driven, inspired, eager to do our best, and make it up and down the mountain safely. Each one of us had different challenges to over-come. Each one of us rose to the challenge individually. Each one of us accepted the responsibility of being in the backcoun-try, and the challenges that come with it. Each one of us had the courage to look within.

Rather than looking for outside influences as to why we couldn't reach our goal, such as weather, terrain, or equipment, we real-ized we were the key to making it happen. We couldn't stop acknowledging how happy we were, up there on the mountain, alone in the wilderness, surrounded by such beauty. We suc-ceeded, individually, and as a team.

Reflections:

Are you feeling frustrated with the progress you are making toward your goal?

Is the key to better communication in your personal relation-ships more patience or more quality time together? As I mentioned earlier, all of these factors are important, but the real key to success is YOU!

Rather than looking for outside influences to blame, are you looking honestly at yourself and at how you are living your life?

Is there a gap between what you say you want in your life and the actions you're taking, or not taking?

THE TIME TO ACT IS TODAY

*"Take time to deliberate, but when the time for action has arrived,
stop thinking and go in."*
~ Napoleon Bonaparte, French political leader

As I am writing this, my son is working on his world history project. He is supposed to create a new country identified by longitude and latitude, a description of the country's climate and identification of the geography and natural resources. It looks like quite a fun project, which stimulates creativity and is based on material covered in class.

At the same time, I am reflecting back on a conference of a Human Resource consortium that I attended. In one of the breakout sessions, we were supposed to imagine the work environment in the year 2020 and come up with ideas as to how to develop employees to meet the demand by then.

It struck me that my son will be 25-years-old in 2020, and he will be at the beginning of his career. What will he need to succeed in tomorrow's world?

It makes me think of the video *Shift Happens*, which has been viewed about 3 million times on You Tube. This video, put together by a high school teacher in Colorado, takes a really big picture view of how rapidly changes will occur in the next few years. Just the fact that the information available to us will double every 72 hours is alarming. For my son to memorize anything seems sort of pointless. It seems to me, that we are moving away from a knowledge based society, and that soon, the facts will all be readily available everywhere, any time.

The video also shows an eye-opening view of globalization. Globalization is real, here and now. Sometimes it seems as if our thinking has not quite caught up yet. We used to think that we needed to develop and protect our own resources in our own country, whichever country we considered ours. Now, we are using resources from around the world; oil from the Middle East, copper from Chile, and natural gas from Russia.

The same development can be observed when we look at manufactured goods. The U.S. used to produce cars domestically for domestic consumption. Now, cars are produced in many different countries for consumption around the world. I just purchased a new iMac computer online from Apple in Palo Alto, California, but the product was shipped directly from the factory in China. It arrived on my doorstep within 5 days of ordering it.

A similar trend is taking place in Human Resources. Employees are increasingly sourced globally. We have all observed the outsourcing of call centers to India, and the Philippines. Some of those call centers have moved back to the US, but at the same time, research and development is now moving out to India.

Work demands and environments, in conjunction with new technologies, will change the way we do things on a daily basis, and we won't be able to stop it. All we can do is adapt to the change as best as possible. Just watch a 14-year-old send a text message, while listening to his ipod, and working on his homework, and you will know what I mean.

I believe it will become increasingly important to focus on what we can control, and what really matters. In order to accomplish that, we need to be clear about our values and doing what's right for humanity. There will be many opportunities to go astray, but with integrity, and a clear sense of direction, we will find our way - and so will our kids. It will be up to us to guide them on this journey, and show them how to take an active role in making a difference for humanity on a daily basis.

I want to invite you to take an active part in this process. Change will take place whether we are sitting on the sidelines or not. We might as well see how we can shape the future by the actions we take today.

Reflections:
What will you do today that will have a traceable, positive impact in the future?
What will you look back on in 2020 that you will be proud of?
What gift are you giving the children who will enter the work force in 2020?
What will you act on today?

WHO DO YOU HAVE TO BE TO MAKE IT HAPPEN?

"Happiness is not an accident. Nor is it something you wish for.
Happiness is something you design."

~ Unknown

We all have the best intentions when we start the New Year. We want to lose weight, we want to spend more time with our children, we want to travel more, and we want to make more money. But then, the day-to-day activities and old habits catch up with us, and all the intentions end up on the back burner. Does this sound familiar?

Would you like this year to really be different? Are you ready to make significant changes? Are you willing to let go of old behaviors, habits, and beliefs?

Intending to make a change is a start, but not nearly enough. Unless you dig deeper and ask the HOW, WHEN, and WHERE questions as well, your intention is unlikely to become reality.

Let me give you an example:

Maria is happy with her current employer, but feels she could take on more responsibilities. She also wants to raise her income by 20%. How is she going to get 20% more? By what date? What other options are available to make more money? There is no one right answer to this, but unless she thinks about the approach she wants to take, her intention will not become reality. At the end of the year, she will find herself in the same position and with the same salary.

The approach is the plan you have to put in place and the action steps you are going to take to make it happen. In Maria's case it might include conversations with her boss and the human resources department, or It might include taking a seminar or class to become more knowledgeable, just to name a few.

But there is one missing piece. WHO do you have to be to make it happen? Addressing issues you are tolerating on a daily basis, setting strong boundaries, and being clear on your standards is essential. This will give you the energy to accomplish your goals, and demonstrate to the people around you who you are and what you stand for. They will respect you for it.

Reflections:
Make a list of resolutions or changes you want to see in your life. Be specific. Come up with an action plan for each one.

Then ask yourself: Who do I need to be in order to make this plan come to fruition? Do I need to set stronger boundaries about my time? Do I need to say no to others in order to say yes to myself?

EMERGING FROM THE FOG

"Dwell not upon thy weariness, thy strength shall be
according to the measure of thy desire."

~ Arab Proverb

I love downhill skiing. Coming back from a ski trip last weekend, I drove through the San Joaquin Valley in California. For those of you not familiar with the Northern California landscape, the San Joaquin Valley runs through Northern California in a north, south direction, between the Sierra Nevada Mountain Range and the Coastal Mountain Range.

Starting out in the Sierra Nevadas, it was a sunny and warm day - absolutely picture perfect. We were listening to fun music and my children were sitting in the back seat chatting away. The mood was light, happy, and very upbeat. Driving through the hilly countryside our hearts seemed to almost jump for joy. Then I pointed at the horizon to make the kids aware of what we were driving into. The valley was covered in a dense layer of fog; locals often refer to it as *Tule Fog*. We were joking about how interesting and clearly defined it looked. As we drove down the hill into the fog, however, our moods instantly changed. The kids quieted down considerably, even the upbeat music didn't sound as fun anymore. Everything was gray and dreary looking. All the colors that we had adored before, seemed to have vanished. It was almost depressing. I automatically turned up the heat in the car, because it seemed much colder, although of course it wasn't. The dense fog made it difficult to imagine we had just been driving through sunshine, and that the sun was shining somewhere at this exact time. I made a point of driving straight through the valley, the most direct route possible, but it seemed to take forever. As we approached the Coastal Mountain Range on the other side of the valley, the fog seemed a bit lighter, and as we drove up the hill, streaks of sunlight were forcing their way through the fog. It was an incredibly uplifting experience. Soon we were immersed in beautiful sunshine.

It struck me that I had experienced something within a couple of hours that many of us experience over a period of months, or even years. Let there be no mistake, I have been there too. We are all on a journey, and life seems to be going along just fine. Then, we seem to lose sight of where we are going. We are maneuvering ourselves into the fog. Life becomes disorienting, confusing gray, and depressing. We don't have a clear road map or sense of direction, and we are somewhat depressed and feel stuck. We cannot imagine that life will ever be sunny again. We also believe we are the only ones in the fog because we can't see anyone. We get lonely, frustrated, and tired. We don't realize that we are transitioning, if not transforming, to a new level in life.

Reflections:
Where do you want to be?
How can you get there?
What do you need to do to get there? Whose help can you solicit?
What will help you visualize the light on the other side of the fog?

LIFE'S PEAKS AND VALLEYS

"A journey of a thousand miles must begin with a single step."

~ Chinese Proverb

When you were a child you probably had dreams of what your life would be like. As a kindergartener you might have dreamed of being a fireman, and as a teenager you probably wanted nothing more than to cut the cord from your parents and prove you independence. As a young adult you might have dreamed of prince charming or a brilliant career changing the world. As you march through life though, you recognize that the path to happiness that you laid out for yourself, is not as straight as you hoped. You find yourself transitioning to college, to marriage, and to having children. As long as these transitions are happy in nature, we are very capable of dealing with them. But then there are the not so happy transitions, such as rejection, divorce, unemployment, illness, and loss of loved ones. Life gets messy and chaotic. Life is like a ride through the country with peaks and valleys. There are highs that are elating and fun, and then there are lows where everything seems to fall apart, and fear seems to drive every move. The only way to get through this unsettling and often scary time, is by recognizing what is, accepting it, and taking action in the form of baby steps - one foot in front of the other; one email, one phone call, and one conversation at a time. As you take those baby steps you move through the valley and up another mountain. It seems a difficult and treacherous path. But if you have ever hiked up a mountain, you know all the pain and suffering to climb it is worthwhile after you see the view from the top. All pain and suffering seems forgotten and all you can see is a clear view of what lies ahead.

As a nation, we seem to be in one of those valleys. Trouble is seemingly everywhere. As I write this, tomorrow marks a most historic inauguration of the first black president of the United States. For many, this is a symbol of hope, a realization of a dream, and now Obama has an almost impossible job ahead of him. As I write this I have not heard his inauguration speech yet, but I am certain it will include a call for action. All of us need to help take those baby steps this nation needs. And we, as individuals, need to take those baby steps that lead us out of our own personal valleys. Yes, there undoubtedly will be suffering, and some hardships, but as long as we keep the ultimate goal, the top of the mountain, the dream alive, we will get there, one step at a time. And along the way you will say: Life is good!

Reflections:
Where are you personally in terms of your life's peaks and valleys?
What is the dream you personally are marching toward?
What is the next baby step you need to take?
What will your contribution be to the baby steps the nation, and in fact the world needs to take to assure freedom, peace, equality and a sustainable planet for all?

WHAT WILL YOU TRY FOR THE FIRST TIME?

"You may be disappointed if you fail, but you are doomed if you don't try."

~ Beverly Sills, American opera singer

In reflecting on the past few months, I recognized a pattern that I hadn't seen before, and I want to share it with you. I have embarked on many *firsts* recently, and upon reflection, many of my clients have done the same thing. Some examples are (as unlikely as some of them might seem):

First time to climb up Half Dome
First time kayaking
First time playing baseball
First time hiring a virtual assistant
First time joining a biking group
First time sky diving
First time becoming an entrepreneur
First time moving out of the country, state, away from home
First time saying NO to someone in particular
First time to speak in front of a large audience
First time allowing yourself to do what you really want, no matter what others say

The list goes on. It doesn't seem easy to do something for the first time, because it is new and unknown. We are afraid of failure, of being rejected, and of being judged, but once we find the courage within ourselves to take a chance, we gain self-confidence, self-esteem, and an incredible boost in energy. As scary as it might seem at first, the gain far outweighs the cost. I now find myself asking: What do I want to try next (that I have never tried before)? I find it stimulating to research how to best go about taking action and add the necessary skills and tools into my toolbox. Once I am ready and prepared, it's a matter of trusting that I have done everything in my power to do my best, and then, with a leap of faith, I go for it! I am really enjoying the process as well as the excitement of accomplishing what I set out to do.

So, what will YOU try for the first time in the next 30 days?
Set a long-overdue boundary?
Start learning an instrument, a sport, and a language?
Hire someone for a task you don't want to or don't have the time to do?
Travel someplace you have never been before?
Join a professional group?
Buy a house, an investment property, and a partnership interest?
Just think of the possibilities.
Congratulations to all of you have recently tried something new. Keep up the fun!

THE MEDICINE WHEEL

"The good neighbor looks beyond the external accidents and discerns those inner qualities that make all men human and, therefore, brothers."
~ Martin Luther King, Jr., *Strength to Love*

I recently had the privilege to accompany my daughter's class on a backpacking trip west of Yosemite National Park. It was a fun-filled week of river walking, hiking, exploring, and learning.

One of the exercises the wilderness expert and naturalist, Kim Powell, took the children through was a ritual involving a medicine wheel. A medicine wheel is simply a way of making a sacred space more real and more visible, by creating a pattern on the ground out of rocks. Ancient people believed that the medicine wheel in itself had great power, and helped create change and healing. Medicine wheels were found throughout history in almost every culture.

Kim had the entire group seated in a circle. She proceeded to tell us about the animals on the medicine wheel. To the east is the deer, a very social animal that likes to be in a pack. To the south is the mouse, which is close to the ground and sees all the detail. The mouse is quite organized and detail oriented. To the west is the bear, opposite of the deer. The bear occasionally hangs out with another bear, but generally likes to retreat and be on his own. To the north, opposite of the mouse, is the eagle. The eagle flies high in the sky and has great vision, and is able to see the big picture. After this explanation, the children were encouraged one by one, to break a piece off a long stick that was passed around, and place the piece of stick on the medicine wheel where they saw themselves. Some of the children considered themselves deer, because they liked to hang out with their friends, but others felt comfortable with the image of the bear. Many of the children identified themselves through their social interactions with their friends and family. They showed that the community around them greatly influences how they see themselves as people.

Interestingly, the adults in the group had a very different perspective on evaluating their place in the medicine wheel; it was a continual cycle that was constantly changing through our ages. Adults seemed to attribute different stages in their lives to different animals. Many expressed that their youth was a more social period, and they considered themselves deer. However, later in life, they became more detail oriented or visionary, and currently think of themselves as mice or eagles.

The exercise helped the children understand more about themselves, but also about their peers in the group. They recognized how it is okay to feel like a bear and request alone time if they need it. I have lived through certain phases in my life and in order to become complete, I really need to live through all stages at some point in order to gain perspective of all the points of view.

Reflections:
What animal do you identify yourself with and where on the medicine wheel were you in the past?
What animals do your family members and friends identify with?
What stages are you lacking perspective in?

WHAT DO YOU WANT TO EXPERIENCE?

"Once we believe in ourselves, we can risk curiosity, wonder, spontaneous delight, or any experience that reveals the human spirit."

~ e e cummings, American poet

My daughter Susie participated in an annual track and field event hosted for local students. After the event her physical education teacher asked the participants to write a reflection of their experience. When she read it to me, I was in awe of her positive attitude and her ability to reflect deeply on what was most important to her about the event. Following is an unedited version of what she wrote, printed with her permission (Liza and Elizabeth are participating classmates):

The Events of Experience

"The Soquel International Games are an annual event where young middle schoolers compete in different sports — whether it be individual or team effort. This year, being the 32nd, we, the sixth grade at Mount Madonna School, went to try our hardest, and that's what we did.

I competed twice: once in the running long jump, and once in the mile. When preparing for the games, my training was hard. But going out there and doing it was even harder. Both sports I enjoyed, and I enjoyed them through the events, too. The running long jump was my deepest love, because I knew I was very good at it, as good as my inspirational figure, Liza. The first time I tried was in the gym, and everyone started talking about how good I was, and immediately ranked me with the best of our class, which was almost embarrassing for my first time. I was always practicing, and I normally got about nine feet when I soared in the air, until my performance. I felt like a bird, that's all I can say. I flew ten feet six inches, which was highest in my class, though Liza didn't compete. I wished she had, because I would have been so proud of her. But, the winner girl went about twelve feet, so I wasn't that close, though I tried. What I really found amazing was the boy winner jumped fifteen feet, an insane number!

I also ran the mile, so for preparation, I would practice once, sometimes twice a day. The first time I tried, I remember, I could not find my running rhythm. One breath per two steps, one breath per four steps. I felt blind trying to run at different breaths each time, so I was slow, and stopped several times during the run. It took me 11:46, which I was not happy about. I knew already that the girls at the games would run in about six minutes, because I had watched last year when Liza ran it and was sweating her butt off. Liza helped me a lot, because she was the one who understood how it felt to be in such a difficult race and I felt her support for when I was doing it. So, with practice, my time got better and better, and I found my breathing rhythm: three steps per breath. Soon, I was waltzing the mile, which I had never planned on. Now, the real race was something different, and Elizabeth, my only companion, dropping out was not expected. The sad part was Elizabeth had only half of a lap to go before she finished, which made me feel sorry. And once we were done, both of us were crying, me because of the pain of leaving her behind, and her because of the pain of Asthma. But I felt proud because I finished, and before three other people, also. It didn't matter that the gold, silver, and bronze metals were going to other people who got to the finish line first, it mattered that I had a heart for Elizabeth, for the sport, and for myself.

So, in total, my running and jumping was for myself and for the work, but not for the praise. I didn't care what people thought of me, because I felt proud I had run a mile, and jumped almost 11 feet. And I'm sort of glad I didn't win anything, because I really wasn't there for that. I was there for the experience, and, boy, I got exactly that!"

Thank you, Susie, for your insights and your great positive attitude. Keep up the Great Spirit!

Reflections:
What do you do when you care what people think about you?
    How come?
What do you feel proud of?
What are you really in the game for?
What do you want to experience?

PRIORITIZING IMPORTANCE

"In order to gain knowledge, add something every day.
In order to gain wisdom, get rid of something every day."
~ Lao Tzu, Chinese philosopher

No matter how much you feel in control of your life, plan events, and feel you are on a roll, sometimes things turn out differently than you expected. I wrote these words recently and little did I know that soon, I would have to follow my own advice. I had just returned from Germany three days previously and was still jet lagged when I received a phone call informing me that due to torrential rains, the basement of our house in Germany, which I had just carefully cleaned and closed down, was about 5 feet under water. Even though I had a fully booked calendar for that week, I decided to cancel all my appointments and fly back to Germany. On the long flight over, I tried to prioritize in my mind what was most important to me and what I wanted to save: photographs, family heirlooms and legal documents. When I arrived at the house, I was shocked. Even though our neighbors (with the help of the fire department) had already pumped the water out, everything up to the level of the light switches was soaked, and it already smelled very strong. The list of affected items included computers, printers, fax machines, a copier, furniture, the furnace, the washing machine and many personal belongings. The legal documents, which were destroyed, turned out to be replaceable, but it took some time to call all the companies and Government offices to have the documents reissued. Having a list of all companies, relevant policy numbers, as well as contacts and phone numbers, proved to be invaluable.

<u>Lesson 1</u>
Have a list of all vital legal documentation, which is updated yearly and kept in a secure (fire and water proof) location.

The family heirlooms turned out to be all right for the most part. Most of them are wooden Christmas ornaments, which have been in the family for many years, and they mean a lot to me. Wood is surprisingly water resistant! I now have them stored in the attic!

<u>Lesson 2</u>
Don't store emotionally valuable items in the basement, where they can get wet feet!

The photographs in photo albums had been placed high enough on the bookcase that they weren't affected. But two plastic containers filled with photographs and negatives taken prior to 1994 were soaked. I have to admit I've never taken the time to deal with them.

<u>Lesson 3</u>
Tolerations, issues that you are putting up with and not addressing, will come back to haunt you, so, deal with them now!

Now, let me return to the topic of priorities. I ended up looking at and drying every single photograph (and there were plenty). Some were destroyed and most were damaged but still acceptable. I found it interesting how easy it was to decide which photographs to keep and which to throw out: Photographs of castles, landscapes and flowers were tossed (I couldn't remember

where they were taken anyhow). However, photographs of relatives and friends were kept. Pictures of apartments, or houses
I had lived in, as well as cars I had driven, seemed worthwhile
keeping (to show the historical change). After I was done, my
brother, his wife and myself had some great laughs seeing how
we had changed over the years. Some humor in the midst of
the mess seemed to help. Because these photographs were
all mixed up, I had decided to keep them in a box, which I can
pull out from time to time and share with family and friends. I
am already excited about this prospect. It seems more fun than
looking through photo albums.

<u>Lesson 4</u>
Handle your photographs as soon as you get them developed,
throw away bad ones, file good ones, and give some away, and
store the negatives in a secure place. Also, remember that digital photographs on computers might not be safe either! (My
computer went belly up!) When people have to evacuate their
homes in an emergency, they often want to take photographs
with them. Are you prepared to do that in an instant?

More important than any of the material things I talked about
are the people who are willing to help you when you are in need.
Even before I left the U.S. to try to salvage items in the flooded
basement, people called to take our children or help in any
other way. After I got to Germany my dad picked me up, and
with my brother and his wife, we cleared the entire basement in
two days. My dad was seventy three at the time and a two-time
cancer survivor. He carried heavy loads as if he was still twenty.
My brother owns his own retail store and he organized someone else to cover for him. His wife, usually quite busy raising

five children and working part time, managed to get coverage for the children and helped out. Our housekeeper loaned us a trailer, which was in high demand. Neighbors offered wheelbarrows, the use of their washing machines and their showers. Contractors came quickly when called and were generous with time and resources. When you are in need, people get closer together and they help - selflessly. The support was wonderful and very welcome. I wonder What stops us from being this close and supportive in our daily routine?

Reflections:
What is most important to you in and around your home?
What action do you need to take to secure your most precious belongings?
What is bothering you in and around your home that you want to make a priority?
In an emergency, what do you want to secure the most?

DECISION MAKING

"A peacefulness follows any decision, even the wrong one."

~ Rita Mae Brown, American writer

Many of my clients asked me about my recent vacation, and I responded by saying: "The universe has been talking to me." Let me explain: We had plans to fly to Germany for a week, but our plans changed when our daughter came down with the flu a few days prior to our scheduled departure. Two days later our son was also lying in bed with a fever spiking at around 104 degrees Fahrenheit. We canceled our flights and prepared for a mellow Christmas at home. Unfortunately, we had some severe storms and I discovered that I had a leak in my roof right above my furnace, which resulted in the heater shutting down. The roofer I called refused to get on the roof while it was wet, so no heat for about 2 weeks. Two days later an electricity pole snapped at the bottom of the hill, and with live wires hanging down, we weren't allowed to pass on foot, or by car, and we didn't have any power in the house either. We were pretty fed up with the situation by then, but the challenges didn't stop there. We decided to make the best of it and escape to a cabin in the mountains. As soon as we arrived, another storm hit, dumping about 2 feet of snow. Again, knocking out our power. This time at an outside temperature of 17 degrees Fahrenheit - brrrr! Next was a dead battery and being stopped by a Highway Patrol Officer for having too much snow on our car. Enough yet? I am sparing you all the little details that went wrong along the way.

Why am I writing about all of these mishaps? Each one of them individually would have been no big deal. All of them happening at once really made me think. I had my unhappy moments about all of them, but I was really wondering and listening. It felt as if the universe was talking to me, I just didn't understand what it was saying. So, I kept asking myself: "What do I need to do differently?" And all of a sudden I realized that my mind had been occupied with some big decisions for years. I had put them on the back burner. I had not avoided making those decisions; I had simply decided not to decide. And I realized that making those decisions would have meant letting go of something big, I had not been ready, or able, to let go of it.

It dawned on me that by holding on, I didn't have more. I had less - less freedom, less joy, less peace of mind, less fun, and even less money.

I decided to let go of not one, but two big beliefs that had been very important to me emotionally. It felt great! It opened up a variety of opportunities that weren't available before. It felt as though I was stepping out of the shadow into the light. What a wonderful feeling! All the mishaps of the prior two weeks, that had drained my energy, were unimportant and I felt totally energized. It catapulted me into a different dimension, a different framework from which to operate. What a giant leap! So much for my conversation with the universe.

Avoidance and denial are keeping you from your best life. I hereby challenge you to have the courage to make tough decisions and take some risks. The rewards outweigh the costs.

Reflections:
What decisions are you avoiding or what are you denying?

What do you need to let go of?

Don't limit yourself to let go of materialistic things, such as cars or homes, but also what beliefs, assumptions, etc. do you need to let go of?

What's holding you back?

What's keeping you awake at night?

WHAT DO YOU WANT?

"If you limit your choices only to what seems possible or reasonable,
you disconnect yourself from what you truly want,
and all that is left is a compromise."
~ Robert Fritz, American author

Have you asked yourself that question lately? On a superficial note, you might have answered yourself saying, *I want more time*, or *I want less stress*, or *I want a better job*, or *I want a loving relationship*. But do you know what you really want, deep down inside? Maybe it's a dream you have had for a long time. But you talked yourself out of it, because it seemed impossible, impractical, too expensive, and so forth. Maybe it's a longing for something in the back of your mind, and you can't really identify what it is. Maybe it is this *intuition* that there is something missing and you don't know what it is.

Several years ago, my children asked me for a pet, ideally a dog. As much as I like dogs (I grew up with Airedale Terriers and English Cocker Spaniels), I couldn't see how to fit a dog into our lifestyle. There were many excuses to not get a dog, the most important being that we travel to Germany on a regular basis (to keep contact with family and friends). I couldn't see traveling with a dog as a good solution.

Being a single mom didn't really help in the decision-making process. Each day posed a multitude of demands as it was. Also, there was no particular breed that I found myself drawn to—Until I walked into a bookstore about a year ago. On one of the counters, I saw a book about dog breeds and it was open to a page about flat-coated retrievers. I had never heard of the breed, but I immediately knew, that if I were to ever have a dog, it would be this kind. I was immediately drawn to this animal with a beautiful black, silky coat and a genuinely loyal face.

In hindsight, I was sold on getting a dog that minute, even though I didn't want to believe it for a while longer. It was on my mind though, because I started talking with friends and family about getting a dog and what changes it would bring. The biggest obstacle was still what to do with the dog, when I was traveling. Then, I mentioned my dilemma to a friend of mine, who was excited about the possibility of dog sitting my dog, while I was gone. She checked it out with her family and said yes. All of a sudden traveling didn't seem to be an excuse anymore. Having a dog became a possibility. And then I realized that it wasn't the kids anymore. It was me. I wanted a dog. I had many flashbacks to my childhood, where I had enjoyed great companionship with our dog, *Gypsy*. I remembered how I had told him everything, and how he would always sit and listen. I started researching breeders.

Shortly later, my children and I drove up to South San Francisco to pick up our black flat-coated retriever puppy, named *Pepper*. On the way home, with the puppy in his arms, my 6-year-old son said: "I can't believe my dream came true." I had made the right decision, no matter how much work was ahead. It was already worth it. Not only was I fulfilling my own dream, but also the dream of my children.

Why am I writing about a dog? Well, the story serves as a reminder to all of us. Dreams can come true. Let's not shut them out by letting our excuses take over. Instead, look for opportunities, listen to your intuition, and talk with friends about your desires. The more you talk about it, the more real it becomes in your mind. It is our own mind that keeps us from fulfilling our dreams.

Ask yourself:

What do I really want?
What have I always dreamt of, but never acted on?
What reason do I have for not acting on it?
What would make it possible?
Once you know which dream you want to have come true, start talking with people about it. Use those around you as resources. Everyone has ideas and suggestions, as to how to overcome excuses and obstacles. The right solution will arrive. It might take some time, but keep at it. The reward is awesome.

ARE YOU PREPARED?

"One never knows what each day is going to bring.
The important thing is to be open and ready for it."
~ Henry Moore, English artist

Have you ever noticed how the universe tends to send you messages, sometimes during the most inopportune times? I have several clients in the technology securities business who are telling me about their frustrations with people not willing to spend time, and money, unless disaster strikes. It's human nature, people don't change their diets until they have had a heart attack. They don't have an emergency plan and kit until hit by an earthquake, fire or flood. They don't back up their data, protect their business from security trouble, or establish good tech support until something goes wrong. I have experienced significant email interruptions in my business recently. Let me extend my sincere apologies to all the readers who have been effected. Here are the lessons I learned. Perhaps they will help you take preventative steps to assure your business continues to run smoothly and problem-free.

1. Establish reliable trusted relationships with people who can support your business/life. Think of it as a team sport.

2. Establish organized and secure record keeping of valuable data. Just like you don't want to scramble for the right phone number when disaster strikes, you want to be able to provide the right passwords and codes when your tech systems are ailing.

3. Keep it simple! I can't emphasize this enough. How often do our minds lead us down rabbit holes? A mere forwarding of

email addresses contributed considerably to my recent trouble. When possible, go the direct, simple path.

4. Observe your own thought process - not from within your mind, but from the outside. Are you reacting to the situation? Are you able to take a step back and respond, calmly and collectedly?

5. Give back when you can. I have spoken with at least a dozen people during my problem solving venture, some more helpful than others, some available when needed, and some not. The ones who ultimately contributed to the solution and completion, were graced with a special *thank you* in form of an email or a testimonial for their business. They made my day. The least I can do is to take a few minutes of my time to thank them, and acknowledge their contribution and impact.

6. Invest time and money in prevention and maintenance to feel more in control. Regular wellness check ups with your doctor, firewalls and antivirus and spam protection, as well as disaster preparedness kits not only save you money down the road, more importantly, they give you peace of mind.

Reflections:
Who do you have on your team for computer support, health care, and disaster relief?
What records and data do you need in order to feel and be prepared?
What processes and systems can you simplify?
What do you need in order to observe your own thinking?
Who can you give back to?
Who has made your day today?

ARE YOU GOING TO TAKE THE RISK OTHERS NEVER WILL?

"If you want a guarantee, buy a toaster."

~ Clint Eastwood, American actor

"Hi everyone!

I'm Dany's daughter, Susie. I go to Mount Madonna School, an hour away from home. For the next school year, I'll be in Lugano, Switzerland, attending TASIS, a boarding school. I'll be away from family and friends long enough to grow apart from them, throw myself into new surroundings and relationships, and have to adapt to a completely different culture.

I have to admit that I'm ridiculously excited. I'll probably pick up snippets of Italian, since the school is in that part of Switzerland. I imagine we'll hang out a lot in town, chatting, sipping coffee, and doing homework. There will be numerous trips, also, to close areas in Europe, which I can't wait for. I hear that they're very supportive academically and that friends are easily made. I'm basically jumping up and down right now; this is going to be so much fun.

Because my mom is a coach, and helps people with decisions like this on a daily basis, it's not hard to imagine that she's been a big help. Not only has she been helping me to prepare for such an adventure, she's also been so understanding of my situation. From Germany, you could tell that we both love European culture more than anything, so she's just as excited as I am about it. Many of my friends really don't understand why I would want to leave California, and there for aren't so very supportive.

My mom gets it and knows how hard it is to choose to be different.

My point is, I'm taking a huge risk. When I get stuck in my routines, I tend to feel too safe, and this is putting myself out there. from being in High School, I know that the easy way out is to conform to peers. A lot of people my age look like they came out of the same mold. So, of course, it's way too hard to purposely pave my own path miles away. Courage is scarce in that area, especially with teens.

I'm here to say that I'm proud of myself for being the person I want to be. I'm not letting anyone else tell me what I want; I'm too busy heading out and grabbing it. By going for it like that, I'm not only doing what I want regardless of what others have to say, but I'm making the statement: I'm willing to take the risks others never will."

Susie Bryan

HANDLING STRESS OR GIVING INTO IT

"It is how people respond to stress that determines whether
they will profit from misfortune or be miserable."

~ Mihaly Csikszentmihalyi, *Flow: The Psychology of Optimal Experience*

The effects of the current financial crisis are felt globally. We are living in fast changing times. Nothing seems stable; everything is in flux—financial markets, and the job market, The media is doing its part to stir up insecurity, and yet security is what people around the world seem to be craving. Lack of security is a form of stress, which is difficult to handle. Following are my top 5 ways of how to handle the stress:

1. Focus your attention on <u>what you can control</u> first

We don't have control over the ups and downs of the stock market, but we do have control over how we spend our money. We have control over our expenses, but not our income. We can affect our income through the actions we take, but we can't control our income. We also have control over how much we subject ourselves to the media coverage we listen to. I spent last weekend in the mountains only getting the bare essential news, which worked well for me.

What can you control right now?

2. <u>Go back to the basics</u>

Tried and true principles in money management, job search, management, relationship building and, even cooking still apply. Simplify and focus on quality, instead of quantity.

What can you simplify?

3. <u>Be grateful</u>

Remind yourself of all the blessings you have. Life can be complicated and challenging in so many different ways. And yet we have plenty of things to be grateful for.
What are you grateful for?

4. <u>Practice extreme self-care</u>

During stressful times, we tend to go into overdrive to compensate for what's challenging us. Consciously decide how to best take care of. You are not doing anyone any good if you are not at your best yourself.

What do you need most to feel whole and complete? Time for yourself, some pampering, a boundary set, a sounding board? Extreme self-care will help you weather the storm.

5. <u>Prioritize and Let Go</u>

Are you getting drowned by the daily rut, i.e. email, news, chores, paper pushing, etc? Ask yourself what matters most in your life right now. What is most important? Everything else can wait for another day. It's okay to say NO!

ARE YOU PUSHING TOO HARD?

"I love climbing. It's a great way to be in nature. It's not just a physical thing; it's also a spiritual thing, where time stops. You stop thinking about stuff. There is no past, present or future. It all disintegrates."

~ Chris Sharma, American rock climber

My children's school invited the school community to attend a slide and video presentation by Chris Sharma, America's Greatest Rock Climber. He happens to be a former student of the school, and, at age 22, has traveled the world climbing rocks. I didn't really know what to expect. I had never heard of Chris Sharma and I didn't know much about rock climbing. I was in for an inspiring treat.

After introducing us to some spectacular photographs of him hanging upside down and becoming one with the rock, he told us about his fascination with a particular rock formation in the South of France. The thought of climbing this rock occupied his life for 4 years. He traveled to France for the first time when he was 16, attempting to climb the blue rock, which had never been successfully climbed before. *Successfully,* in rock climbing terms, means climbing the entire rock in one go without ever falling. Chris did wear a harness every time, but falling could easily mean falling 40 to 50 feet. He traveled to France three times, each time camping close to the rock attempting to climb it nearly every day. The entire rock is a 30-degree overhang and the hardest part is near the top. Chris described how he fell 30 to 40 times, always at the same spot, close to reaching his goal. He had a mental block, almost anticipating the fall once he got to that spot. He described his frustration and his determination to try again, and again.

Then one day, he decided to try the rock again, despite not being at his best. His muscles were sore from his previous attempts, and he felt fatigued. He hiked to the rock and started climbing. He was sure he wouldn't make it that day, but something strange happened. When he got to the crucial spot that day, he had let go of his expectation to make it to the top. Much to his surprise, he had freed the energy to go beyond the difficult spot. He made it to the top! He had tried so hard for so long, but only when he was no longer attached to the outcome, did he succeed.

Often we try hard to come up with a solution, to make a decision, or to reach a goal. It feels as if we are beating our head against the wall. The harder we push, the worse it gets. Pushing so hard costs a lot of energy and it leaves us exhausted. When we decide to let things go, we break through the barriers that had been stopping us all along. So, where are you pushing too hard, leaving, yourself de-energized? What expectations do you need to let go of? Where are you attached to the outcome?

Just to be clear, I am not advocating, letting go of the goal, even though reevaluation is always good. What I am advocating is for you to explore what is holding you back from reaching your goal. Good luck!

TAPPING INTO UNIVERSAL WISDOM

"We don't receive wisdom; we must discover it for ourselves
after a journey that no one can take for us or spare us."
~ Marcel Proust, French thinker

The world is full of unrest, hurricanes, floods, wars, hunger, AIDs, terror, and the list goes on. All of us are affected by this instability, directly or indirectly. Even though we cope on a day-to-day basis, what's happening in our world leaves us feeling unsettled, to say the least. How to deal with the challenges seems to often divide, rather than connect, us. We seem to be in need of some uplifting experiences in order to manage the difficulties we face as individuals, nations, and the world.

I recently had a wonderful reminder as to how to tap into our universal wisdom and create feel-good experiences. Let me be more specific. While in Germany this summer, I found myself in front of the CD section of a department store. I remembered a recent Public Broadcasting Special, featuring Andrea Bocelli. For those of you who don't know him, he is an Italian opera and pop singer with a beautiful voice. I found a CD called Bocelli, on which I recognized some of the titles. My children and I listened to the CD in the car on my way home. One song in particular, called 'Con Te Partiro' moved us. None of us understood the lyrics, but that didn't matter at all. We could tell the music came from Bocelli's heart. We discussed what we were feeling and what we were thinking about as we listened to the song. All three of us described the song as very uplifting, happy, and cheerful. That's what it must feel like to fly, A spiral upwards.

I was reminded of my childhood: When I worked on my home-work, and when I listened to AFN, the American Forces Net-work, the only US radio station I had access to. I never found it distracting; I just listened to the music. I didn't speak English at the time, so the lyrics didn't mean anything to me. Even if the songs were about death, or destruction, or love, I couldn't tell the difference. Even today, I find myself tuning out the words and simply feeling the music. Music - the only universal language we all share.

Listening to Andrea Bocelli reminded me that the lyrics of a song can add to a song, but the music can also stand alone. When I find myself getting depressed about what's happening in the world, I listen to music. Sometimes I listen to songs in a foreign language I don't understand, in order to connect to the heart and soul of the artist, through the beauty of the human voice. What a way to connect on a very deep level! It makes me listen with my heart rather than with my head! If you are feeling the blues about what's happening around you, try listening to music. Maybe try listening to a song in a language foreign to you.

We are all connected, so if you are feeling good, everyone around you will feel good as well. What a gift!

WHAT DIFFERENCE CAN YOU MAKE?

"Human beings, by changing the inner attitudes of their minds,
can change the outer aspects of their lives."

~ William James, American philosopher

During a summer trip to Europe, I noticed many more solar panels on Bavarian rooftops than I had ever seen before. Rooftops, slopes, and materials are highly regulated there, in an effort to keep a homogeneous look in a very traditional region. The appearance of an alpine village is deeply rooted in culture and tradition. To see that many solar panels astonished me. Noticing these solar panels was the first example of my heightened awareness. Then I noticed that the car I had leased to drive around Europe, could drive for 800 miles with one tank of fuel. Granted the car was much smaller than my US minivan, but nonetheless, noticed. Considering that fuel prices are at twice the level of the US fuel prices, this fuel efficiency made a huge impact on my pocket book. Then, I had discussions with Europeans, as well as Americans, about recycling habits in different countries. For example our trashcan in Germany holds about 2 cubic feet of trash, which gets picked up every two weeks. Quite a difference from the huge garbage cans I use in California, which get picked up every week. Apparently, I was on a path of noticing more and more environmental issues. Not that I hadn't noticed them before, but I was now looking at each issue from a different perspective.

I have always been concerned about the environment, but more from a perspective of adhering to rules and regulations, for example, being forced to recycle in a certain way.

Two weeks ago, I walked into a bookstore in San Francisco and picked up a book with the title *The Meaning of the 21st Century*, by James Martin. What an eye opener! Never before had I recognized the connection between overpopulation, over fishing, climate change, illiteracy, energy limitations, and new technologies. Not that I hadn't read about these issues before; I believe I am quite well informed about these types of issues - at least no less than the average person. But I had never seen the bigger picture quite like this before. I had never connected the dots and seen the connections between all of these issues.

All of a sudden I started questioning my own motivation about getting involved, or not getting involved. Let me give you an example: When building my barn, I had set everything up to install photovoltaic panels on my roof. I had not seen the incentive to put solar on my roof then, because, due to my very efficient heating system, it would take me years to recuperate the cost and break even. I had only looked at it from a perspective of cost and financial return. Now, I was beginning to look at it from the point of view that we couldn't afford not to install solar panels on every rooftop in order to preserve energy for future generations. Whatever we are using up now, is not going to be available for our kids and grandkids.

I started to think about how I can change the way I do things on a daily basis. Am I single-handedly able to further research about alternative fuels? Probably not. But can I reduce the amount of energy I am using? Absolutely! I talked with a contractor about giving me a quote for the installation of solar panels.

Can I help slow down the destruction of the ozone layer? Absolutely! I have planted more than 20 trees in the last year. The trees will help slow down the destruction of the ozone layer. Can I conserve water? Absolutely! Not only do I have low-flow toilets in my home, but rather than installing a lawn, which needs to be watered regularly, I seeded native grasses that have minimal water requirements and do not need cutting. Also, I am in the process of ordering rain barrels to save rainwater from my rooftop. Can I help prevent the loss of topsoil? Absolutely! I can further improve my composting efforts and amend my soils accordingly. As a result, I will purchase less soil. Can I help with recycling efforts? Absolutely! I have just received several tons of broken concrete blocks from a former driveway (for free I might add!) to build several retaining walls on my property. By doing so, I can create a vegetable garden, and prevent a bunch of concrete from going into a landfill. Can I reduce the amount of trash in our oceans and rivers? Absolutely! My kids and I participated in the annual beach cleanup this month.

By reading the book, I recognized how I can do my part in the success of the 21st century. I have many more ideas and I will start to implement as many as I can. You have to think locally to affect globally. I am trying to do my part, what about you? What can you do today, tomorrow, or this month to make a difference and to make an impact? Maybe you want to start with turning the water off while you are brushing your teeth, or maybe you are a scientist working on developing alternative fuels. Whatever you do and whoever you are, YOU can make a difference!

Reflections:

Write down three things you want to start with and mark them in your calendar. Schedule time to accomplish these goals. You will feel very good by giving your time and expertise to the well-being of this planet and future generations. Stop standing on the sideline and start taking responsibility for all your actions, every day, all day long! Brainstorm with neighbors, friends and family members and see what you can do individually or together.

YOU AS AN ARCHITECT OF CHANGE

"Everything you can imagine is real."

~ Pablo Picasso, Spanish artist

I had attended the annual Women's Conference, hosted by California's First Lady, Maria Shriver. Much like in previous years, the event was inspirational and thought provoking on many different levels. This year's theme was *Architect of Change*. The only thing constant is change. Rather than let change happen around us while we stand still, why not be an architect of change, and proactively change what is no longer working for us? To me this conference was a call, to not only the women present in the auditorium, but, to all women. In fact a call to all of mankind, to be that architect of change. Let me take a bit of a detour for a minute:

A recent landmark UCLA study suggests that *women respond to stress with a cascade of brain chemicals that also cause women to make and maintain friendships with other women.* Apparently, increased levels of oxytocin encourage women to tend to children and gather with other women. While men, with increased production of testosterone under stress, seem to respond with either fight or flight. As it turns out most of the stress research done over the last 5 decades was done on male subjects. The increased oxytocin release in women actually produces a calming effect. Testosterone, which men produce in high levels when under stress, seems to reduce the effect of oxytocin.

I am not a scientist, but the findings of this study seem very plausible to me. We do live in a time of unprecedented change.

Society, technology, economy, jobs, housing, communities, everything seems to be changing rapidly. Change is constant, and as Sir Richard Branson says in his recent book (see book recommendation), change is a threat - and one day it will kill you. Threats, such as change, cause stress. Women respond to stress differently than men. What would our world look like if there weren't only a fight or flight response to the major threats to our planet, countries, and societies, but also a calming one?

For the first time in history, women make up about half of the US workforce. What if half of the work force was to respond to stress differently? In fact it's already happening. And what if half of the workforce were to prioritize differently in stressful situations?

Whenever we look at statistics, the numbers seem to explain everyone else's situation. What about you? What if YOU were to be the architect of change, the one who could make the difference in your community, work environment, or government? Why not you? As a woman you handle stress differently; you might also not be as prone to taking risks. I am advocating for women not to wait for others to be the architect(s) of change. Instead, step up to the plate, take on the leadership role, speak up, and make yourself heard! There is no better time than now.

What frustrates you to no end? What do you not want to tolerate any longer? Where will you get involved and take a stand?

When I hear of unequal pay, increasing sex trafficking, women's rights in Chechnya reversing to the middle ages, and many other forms of oppression towards females, I can't help but think: It's time, time for courage, time for action, time for us to reach out to other women and support them.

If you are a male member of the species, I might have lost you after the first paragraph. But if you are still with me - congratulations! We need your help, if you want your daughters to receive the respect, trust, and equality they deserve.

Let's collaborate and create the world we want our children to live in, by being the architects of change, by means of respecting and trusting each other's skills and strengths.

WHAT OCCUPIES YOUR TIME?

"Time is the most valuable thing a man can spend."

~ Theophrastus, Greek writer

I have been pondering time. What occupies my time? Have you ever asked yourself that question? What is time really? Some think of it as a sequence of moments strung together like pearls in a necklace—each one precious and rare. If time is so precious, why do we treat it so poorly? We race and we hustle from one appointment to the next without giving meaning to the experiences, good and bad, we have along the way. Are we giving time the time of day? Seriously, what occupies your time? Let's think about it. Are you in charge? Are you managing your time, or has automation taken over? We get up, we do our morning routine by getting dressed and having breakfast, we go to work, school and so forth. Those are all automated tasks that are occupying our time. Don't get me wrong, there is a certain beauty to routine, but why not mix it up a little? Isn't that what we do when we go on vacation? Maybe we get up and go for a swim, even before breakfast. Or maybe we write in a journal, or we grab a cup of coffee and go for a walk on the beach. And yet when we are home, we fall into this trap of doing things over, and over, again just because we have done it this way and it feels comfortable. Sticking with the routine has become a habit. Think about your routine and your daily habits. Which activities feel good and feed your soul? Which ones are chores that you do to please others or that irritate you? When do you build in time to reflect, to ponder, and to contemplate about how life is going, what works, what doesn't, what nourishes you and what robs you? I challenge you, no, I urge you to take charge of your time. It's yours for the taking. As we watch our elders pass on and our children grow up, we cannot waste time. This day will never come again!

BECOME A MASTER

"Part of being a master is learning how to sing in nobody
else's voice but your own."

~ Hugh Macleod, American artist

One of my clients was scheduled to give a couple of speeches in front of large audiences of influentials. He was not perceived to be a public speaker by some, in fact, he was introduced before one of the presentations with the words: *xxx is not a public speaker, but he has agreed to do this for us.* Despite this introduction, which tugged on his self-confidence, he gave a 45-minute presentation without the help of any notes, which he received rave reviews for. When asked how he did it, he replied after researching the subject matter thoroughly, That he practiced, practiced, practiced. He rehearsed in front of the mirror, he spoke out loud, and he totally internalized what he was going to say. As it turns out, he used to attend regular Toastmasters meetings and loves public speaking. It energizes him and he loves doing it. (Toastmasters are a non-profit organization dedicated to helping people become more competent and comfortable in front of an audience.)

In our youth we are told to practice piano or go to soccer practice. We rehearse for plays and repeatedly memorize vocabulary. This leads to success in school, sports, or our hobbies.

The same applies to us as adults, but we don't necessarily think of success as a result of practice. Think about something you are currently learning, for example how to negotiate, how to do an effective job search, how to market your business, how to market yourself in your organization, how to speak a foreign language, and how to manage a team. The list is endless. Aren't we all learning all the time? What makes us think we know how to do everything well without practicing? We need to practice our negotiation skills, our management skills, our organization skills, our 30-second elevator speech, or whatever it might be. The fulfillment comes with practice, because we feel good as we become better and stronger.

Reflections:

What are you learning right now that you want to master, or, what do you want to learn that you want to master? Whatever it might be, keep practicing and anticipate that there will be natural plateaus that feel like setbacks. Don't give up. The reward comes when you move through the plateaus and master your subject. Enjoy the practice!

ELIMINATE, DELEGATE AND AUTOMATE

"Time is free, but it's priceless, you can't own it, but you can use it.
You can't keep it, but you can spend it.
Once you've lost it you can never get it back."
~ Harvey MacKay, American writer

I see opportunities everywhere and yet it seems difficult for people to juggle them all. I want to give you an insight into the process I have been going through for a while now; as a matter of fact, it is an ongoing process. The process entails three steps:

1. Elimination
2. Delegation
3. Automation

At regular intervals, weekly, monthly, and quarterly, I list all the opportunities in front of me.

By the way, this process works for corporate executives and entrepreneurs equally as for parents, – in short for everyone.

It is important to be able to identify opportunities in the first place. Once listed, I go through and prioritize them. Which ones are most fun, most promising, or most exciting? Whichever are on the bottom of the list are Often those opportunities that others see for me, but they are just not so exciting to me. I take immediate action and extract myself from the running.

Next, I go through my list of opportunities and delegate to others what I can. Ideally I delegate projects rather than single tasks, and I state the expectation and the standard I want to see upheld. By delegating, I have freed up more time for myself. I can now focus on automating some of my processes, for example, having my bills paid automatically, or having a reminder pop up in my email inbox every time I need to write another newsletter. I have been automating a lot over the course of the past 10 years. I am always amazed as to what else I really can automate. As a result, I don't have to think about things, over and over again. I put focused energy into setting the automation up once, and monitoring it afterwards. Whew, now I have mental thinking space for what really matters to me.

ALLOW YOURSELF TO DE-STRESS

"Acquire inner peace and a multitude will find their salvation near you."

~ Catherine Doherty, Russian social activist

We are living in challenging times. The financial markets are unstable, to put it mildly. News from around the world is scary and the media does its best to fuel the hype. People are either afraid of losing their job, afraid of corporate reorganizations, or afraid of steering their companies through rough waters. In addition, our daily living is affected by rising prices of fuel, food, and just about everything else. Everyone seems to be on edge, and people are stressed.

One feels grateful when not directly affected by the mortgage crisis or flooding somewhere in the world.

I am impressed by my clients, who, despite uncertain environments, find jobs, grow their businesses, stay focused, and keep the momentum going.

For each and every one of us, hard times offer tremendous opportunity. The possibilities are endless, if we are willing to observe and listen.

Following are my top 5 ways to de-stress, regardless of what comes at you. These de-stressors won't cost you a dime and help you weather the storm:

1. Journal
Use the power of writing down, ideally by hand, what is on your mind. The good, the bad, and the ugly—as well as everything

you are grateful for. Feel free to do a brain dump daily, and don't worry about grammar or punctuation. No one but you should read your journal.

2. Be Selective About Media

I was raised with the notion that you need to be informed about what's happening in the world. I actively observe and read newspapers, magazines and broadcasts from around the world. However, I am very selective as to how engaged I get with the news. I get informed, but not sucked in. Sensationalism angers me, so I stay away from it - quite appropriate for a past journalism major. News is a business and it's prudent to keep this in mind as consumers.

3. Focus On What Truly Matters Most

Even if we had 100 hours in a day, we'd still have tasks to finish. As we tackle issues on our to-do lists, we are constantly creating new to-do items. The trick is to focus on what's most important while accepting the letting go of everything else. Not always easy, but doable, and a path to sanity.

4. Set Boundaries Where Appropriate

Often our needs aren't met because someone is invading our boundaries. When did we forget the word no? It's ok to say NO to not being treated respectfully, to another project you really don't have time or energy for, to hundreds of email in your inbox that drain your energy, to the clutter surrounding you, and to yourself for eating food that's not healthy for you. The list is endless. It's time to say no!

5. Treat Yourself Well

A car doesn't run well when the fuel gauge registers empty.

Neither does the human body—physically, emotionally, and spiritually. Nourish your body with healthy food and exercise. Nourish your soul with music, laughter, and nature, and your energy level will go up. Life will look much brighter. Only when your glass is full, are you capable of giving to others.

Good luck staying the course!

WORK TOWARD THE GREATER GOOD

"If we cannot end now our differences, at least we can help
make the world safe for diversity."
~ John F. Kennedy, American president

Having served on the Mount Madonna School Board, I was asked to support the Nominating Committee in finding and selecting nominees for the Board of Directors. While I had conversations with interested parties from different constituents, it was necessary to talk about the expectations that would come with board membership. Unlike some other schools, all board members at MMS are nominated and appointed, not voted in.

Regardless which constituency board members come from, parent, faculty, advisor, and so on, members are asked to leave their *constituent hats* at home and put a *board hat* on. A board member has the responsibility to make decisions that are best for the organization, not for their own personal interest. For example, I personally might not be in favor of a tuition increase, but I might vote for it on the board to assure the financial stability of the school.

Let's translate this concept to the election process. People vote for what's best for them, and not what's best for their community. I think that's sad, but true. This explains all of the special interest groups and earmark discussions. It explains the enormous amount of money spent on, and by lobbyists. What will it take for all of us to leave our personal interests at the door and work together to come up with solutions that work for the well-being of humanity? Ok, I can hear the naysayer already. This is not attainable, because everyone will always look out for himself or herself. Well, see where it got us! It got us to a financial crisis, a crisis of the labor market, and a crisis of our own conscience. What if it was possible? What if by leaving our personal interest to the side, we could avoid crises of the magnitude we have been experiencing? Wouldn't we all feel better about ourselves and the difference we are making? Wouldn't we feel better about the legacy we are leaving behind? Do we really expect to get everything for free? We need to make tough choices and now is the time. I want to ask you to consider leaving your self-interest at the door and do what's right for the greater good. How hard can it be?

Reflections:

Are there situations in your life where you are acting out of self-interest?

Are you listening to the needs, ideas and points of views of others?

Are your decisions made with the greater good in mind?

ACTION

If you haven't taken action yet, it's time!

I use an assessment, called Clean Sweep, with my clients and for myself, at least once a year, to assess my level of balance. You can receive this assessment by emailing us at db@dbcoach.com.

Good luck!

BOOKS

The Seven Habits of Highly Effective People
By: Steven Covey

The Secret
By: Rhonda Byrne

The Power of Now
By: Eckhart Tolle

Blink: The Power of Thinking without Thinking
By Malcolm Gladwell

You Already Know How to be Great
By: Rebecca Merrill

The Art of Non-Conformity
By: Chris Guillebeau

You Had Me at Woof: How Dogs Taught Me the Secrets of
Happiness
By: Julie Klam

Conversations with Myself
By: Nelson Mandela

Women, Food and God: An Unexpected Path to Almost
Everything
By: Geneen Roth

Where Good Ideas Come From: The Natural History of Innovation
By: Steven Johnson

The Success Principles
By: Jack Canfield

Overcoming Underearning
By: Barbara Stanny

Strong Women Stay Young
By: Miriam Nelson

Going Gray
By: Anne Kreamer

Inventing the Rest of Our Lives: Women in Second Adulthood
By: Suzanne Braun

Personal and Executive Coaching: The Complete Guide for Mental Health Professionals
By:Auerbach, J.

Coaching that Counts: Harnessing the Power of Leadership Coaching to Deliver Strategic Value
By: Anderson, D., & Anderson, M.

Developing sustainable leaders through coaching and compassion.
By: Boyatzis, R., Smith, M., & Blaize, N.

Executive coaching for managerial excellence: A roadmap for executives, human resources and coaches.
By: Brenner, M.

The Art of Building People: 36 Coaching Tools for Getting More out of Work and Life
By: Chiodi, M.

Influence Without Authority
By: Cohen A., & Bradford, D.

Good to Great: *Why Some Companies Make the Leap... and Others Don't*
By: Collins, J.

Executive coaching: A perception of the chief executive officers of the most successful fortune 500 companies
By: Fanasheh, S.

Coaching: Evoking Excellence in Others
By: Flaherty, J.

What Got You Here Won't Get You There
By: Goldsmith, M., & Reiter, M.

Emotional Intelligence at Work
By: Goleman, G.

Dialogue: The Art of Thinking Together
By: Isaacs, W.

The Science of Getting Rich: Attracting Financial Success through Creative Thought
By: Wallace D. Wattles

Executive Coaching: Practices and Perspective
By: Catherine Fitzgerald

Coaching for Leadership: How the World's Greatest Coaches
    Help Leaders Learn
By: Marshall Goldsmith

The Anger Trap: Freeing Yourself from the Frustrations that
    Sabotage your Life
By: Dr. Les Carter

How to Speak and Write Correctly
By: Joseph Devlin

The Book of Awakening: Having the Life you Want by Being
    Present in the Life you Have
By: Mark Nepo

The Rules of Life
By: Richard Templar

The Winners Manual
By: Jim Tressel

Success Built to Last: Creating a Life that Matters
By: Porras, Emery and Thompson

Resilience: Reflections on the Burdens and Gifts of Facing Life's
    Adversities
By: Elizabeth Edwards

How to Win Friends and Influence People
By: Dale Carnegie

The Art of Money Getting: Golden Rules for Making Money
By: P.T. Barnum

Strengths Finder 2.0
By: Tom Rath

Getting More: How to Negotiate to Achieve Your Goals in the
Real World
By: Stuart Diamond

Getting Things Done: The Art of Stress-Free Productivity
By: David Allen

How to Survive the End of the World as We Know It
By: James Wesley Rawles

Delivering Happiness: A Path to Profits, Passion and Purpose
By: Tony Hsieh

Drive: The Surprising Truth about What Motivates Us
By: Daniel Pink

The Creative Process of the Individual
By: T. Troward

The Go-Getter: A Story that Tells Us how to be One
By: Peter B. Kyne

WEBSITES

http://www.uncommonforum.com/

http://www.babyboomer-forums.com/index.php

http://www.tips-for-boomers.com/

http://www.boomerater.com/

http://www.instituteofcoaching.org

http://www.thefoundationofcoaching.org

http://www.emcouncil.org

Association for Profession Executive Coaching and Supervision
http://www.apecs.org

http://www.certifiedcoach.org

Society for Human Resource Management
http://www.shrm.org

http://www.wabccoaches.com

http://www.askthecoachexchange.com/

http://www.theholbrowgroup.com/

http://www.michaelstern.com/coaching/index.php

http://exec.actioncoach.com/

http://www.ecoachingsuccess.com/

http://www.todaysleadership.com/

http://www.leadershipcoachinginc.com/

http://www.change-leaders.com/

http://www.coach4growth.com/

Center for Creative Leadership
http://www.ccl.org/leadership/about/index.aspx

Center for Management and Organization Effectiveness
http://www.cmoe.com/

http://www.coachfederation.org/

http://www.coachingconsortium.org/

Women Websites

http://www.change-leaders.com/coaching_executive_women.html

National Association for Women Executives
http://www.nafe.com/?service=vpage/1474

http://www.thechicagonetwork.org/

http://www.boarddirectorsnetwork.org/

http://www.c200.org/

http://www.wexpo.biz//

http://www.catalyst.org/

American Society of Women Accountants
http://www.aswa.org/

American Business Women's Association
http://abwa.org/

National Association of Women Business Owners
http://nawbo.org/

http://executivewomen.org/

Business and Professional Women Foundation
http://bpwfoundation.org/

http://www.advancingwomen.com/

http://womenatworknetwork.com/

National Women's Studies Association
http://nwsa.org/

Women on Wall Street
http://wows.db.com/

NON-PROFITS

http://helpguide.org/

http://www.soulzatwork.com/nonprofit-leadership-program.html

Michael Kumer – Executive Director of Nonprofit Leadership
Institute
http://www.duq.edu/nli/staff.cfm

http://www.coachingforacause.org

http://coachingtheglobalvillage.org/

http://www.educo.org.za/home/default.asp

http://www.coachingcon.org/

http://www.peer.ca/

http://www.peacemakers.ca/

EXPERTS

Shawn Nelson
http://www.mrgoodman.com/

Brian Tracy
http://www.briantracy.com/

Chris Widener
http://www.madeforsuccess.com

Terri Levine
http://www.terrilevine.com/

Joel Garfinkle
http://www.garfinkleexecutivecoaching.com/

Gail Voisin
http://www.gailvoisin.com/

Martin Ramsden
http://www.martinramsden.com/

Tim Redmond
http://www.redmondleadership.org/

Kathy Baker
http://www.yoursuccessmasterynow.com/

Alicia Marie Fruin
http://www.peoplebizinc.com/

Dr. Mary Read
http://powerfulmindcoaching.com/

Barbara Kely
http://www.lifegardeners.com/

Layne Hood
http://laynehood.com/

Barb McEwen
http://www.2020executivewomen.com

Jean Stafford
http://www.jeanstafford.com/

FORI

http://selfhelpmagazine.com/forum/

http://www.topix.com/forum/recent

http://www.uncommonforum.com/

http://www.successandlife.com/forum/

http://andagain.websitetoolbox.com/?forum=1

http://www.thecoachingforums.com/index.php

http://www.thecoachingforums.com/viewforum.php?f=11

http://www.bizymoms.com/forums/

http://www.big-boards.com/

http://www.aimoo.com/

http://forums.ivillage.com/

http://www.thoughts.com/forums/

http://vervecoaching.com/introducing-a-coaching-forum-for-emerging-enterprises/

http://www.thecreativeleadershipforum.com/

http://www.forumofexecutivewomen.com/

http://iwforum.org/

http://www.womens-forum.com/

Daniela Bryan is Owner and Chief Vision Officer of DBCoach, an executive coaching firm, which she founded in 2001. She is an expert at discerning what matters most to CEOs, executive directors, small business owners, business partners, and their teams worldwide.

She has successfully coached senior and international executives, in thousands of coaching hours, to live up to their potential in companies ranging from Audi to Visa, from Citigroup and Microsoft, to Nestle and Toyota. Her breadth of experience in working in, and with, corporations non-profit organizations, small businesses, and start up companies allows her to relate to shift people's perspectives to success.

In her *former* life, she was Director of Marketing Communications and Training for the Eastman Kodak Company in London for Europe, Africa, and the Middle East, following an extensive career in sales, marketing and product management.

Daniela graduated with a BA degree from the USC Annaberg School of Journalism and an MBA degree from Thunderbird School of Global Management. She also graduated from CoachU and currently holds a Professional Certified Coach credential from the International Coach Federation.

Daniela manages a global business and estate, has lived in several countries, and speaks several languages. She is an experienced real estate investor and she has been general contractor for her homes in Germany and in California, where she lives with her two teenage children and dog.

In addition, she finds time to serve on the Board of Directors for Mount Madonna School in Watsonville, California, because she believes in the power of education.

People in her inner circle know her as trustworthy, dependable, and honest. They know she was born in Germany, but recognize her as a truly global citizen.

www.ingramcontent.com/pod-product-compliance
Lightning Source LLC
Chambersburg PA
CBHW072117270326
41931CB00010B/1591